THE KENNEDYS
of
STONE CROSS MANSION

by
Stuart Allison

Pixel tweaks
PUBLICATIONS
ULVERSTON • CUMBRIA

Published in 2014
© Copyright Stuart Allison

ISBN: 978-0-9927514-3-2

Cover and Book Design by Russell Holden
www.pixeltweakspublications.co.uk

Cover painting by Adrian Rawlinson

Printed by Short Run Press, Exeter

All rights reserved without limiting the rights under copyright reserved above, no parts of this publication may be reproduced, stored in or introduced into a retrieval system, or transmitted in any form, or by any means (electronic, mechanical, photocopying, recording or otherwise) without the prior written permission of both the copyright owner and the publisher of this book.

Many photos appear by kind permission from some of the families mentioned on facing page, who have asked that they are not reproduced without seeking prior permission.

Pixeltweaks
PUBLICATIONS
ULVERSTON • CUMBRIA

Acknowledgements

I would like to thank all the people who have helped
compile this account particularly;

Myles & Tom Kennedy of Ulverston

William George Ainslie's grandchildren

Myles W.W. Kennedy, Madeleine Bintley & Marie Barltrop

Charles Adler

Kathleen's grandsons, Michael and Peter Loup

Caroline Draper née Milligan – great grand daughter of Florence Kennedy

Mark Outhwaite great grandson of Arthur Kennedy

Arthur's descendants

Marl International

Adrian & Aida Rawlinson

The Holmes-Higgin Family

Bernadette Calvey

Barrow records office

Northern Lights

Russell Holden

References to *Furness Year Books & Furness Past & Present*
(Tweddell & Richardson).

The author can be contacted at *kennedysofstonecross@gmail.com*

To our father, Bryan Allison
who always threatened to write a book,

To my family for all their support,

And our mother
who has always been the wind beneath our wings.

CONTENTS

THE FAMILY
Chapter 1   Charles Storr Kennedy 1
Chapter 2   The Rowleys 3
Chapter 3   Charles Burton Kennedy 9
Chapter 4   Myles Kennedy 13

THE CHILDREN
Chapter 5   Myles Theodore Burton Kennedy 21
Chapter 6   Wilfred Burton Rowley Kennedy 37
Chapter 7   Marguerite Rowley Kennedy MBE 39
Chapter 8   Alice Storr Kennedy 41
Chapter 9   Elizabeth Burton Kennedy 43
Chapter 10   Florence Campbell Kennedy 45
Chapter 11   Kathleen Kennedy 47
Chapter 12   Mary Maude Kennedy 49
Chapter 13   Alfred Alexander Kennedy 51
Chapter 14   Theobald Walter Butler Kennedy 55
Chapter 15   Violet Kennedy 59
Chapter 16   William George Ainslie Kennedy 61
Chapter 17   Lucy Kennedy 65
Chapter 18   Emma Law Kennedy 66
Chapter 19   Mabel Kennedy 67
Chapter 20   Arthur Herbert Kennedy 69

Chapter 21   Holy Trinity Church 75
Chapter 22   Stone Cross Mansion 77

Stone Cross after the Kennedys 91
Marl & beyond 101
Kennedy coat of arms 113
Coat of arms still found at Fair View 115
Kennedy Gravestones 116
Index 117

INTRODUCTION

My interest in Stone Cross Mansion and the Kennedy family dates back to the 1990s when I first made a visit to the offices of Marl International who were based there at the time.

Up until then I'd never heard of Stone Cross Mansion, but after driving up the long sweeping drive, entering through the main entrance and seeing the great house for the first time I felt I needed to find out more about the family that built it and lived there.

In recent years I've been lucky enough to be involved in repairing and maintaining the building in its current, sorry state and it reignited my interest to find out more.

Stone Cross Mansion lies on the outskirts of Ulverston, Cumbria but formerly came under the district of Osmotherley, Lancashire. The Stone Cross estate was used to house old linen sheds and terraced houses.

I always wonder what consequences a marriage union has on the world and when Myles Kennedy married Margaret Rowley and had 16 children, an exciting journey lay ahead to find out where each of their lives led.

I'm sure Myles and Margaret had a plan set out for each of their offspring, tailored to their individual talents but as the saying goes, 'God laughs at those who make plans', fate was going to intervene.

On March 13th 1883 the Kennedy's world was about to be turned upside down. Myles died suddenly at the age of 47 and the Kennedy family must have wondered, what happens now?

I have tried to follow the path of the children and their families to see where they led, from the time when the family had great wealth and all the trappings that went with it. They had a vast social circle that mixed with Dukes, Lords and pioneers of industry and a large extended family particularly with the Rowleys.

At a time when world conflict was on the horizon, the wars were going to be the making of some and have tragic consequences for others, and like all families living through those times there were mixed emotions of losing loved ones and tales of heroism.

I don't profess to be an author or expert and apologise for any discrepancies contained within the book. Where possible I have tried to stick to facts from newspaper articles, archives and personal family records. A photo album that belonged to Alice Kennedy has provided many photos of the young Kennedys, but as most are not named, quite a bit of deduction has been applied and some cross references may have occurred during identification.

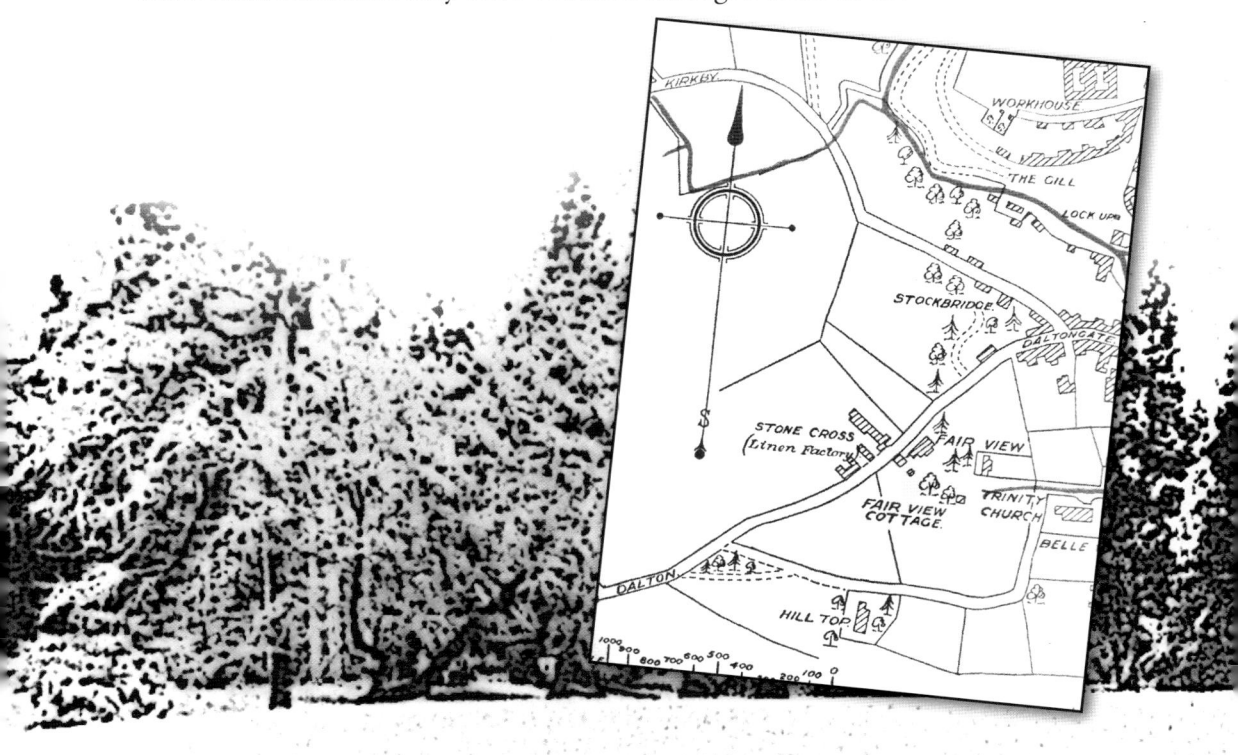

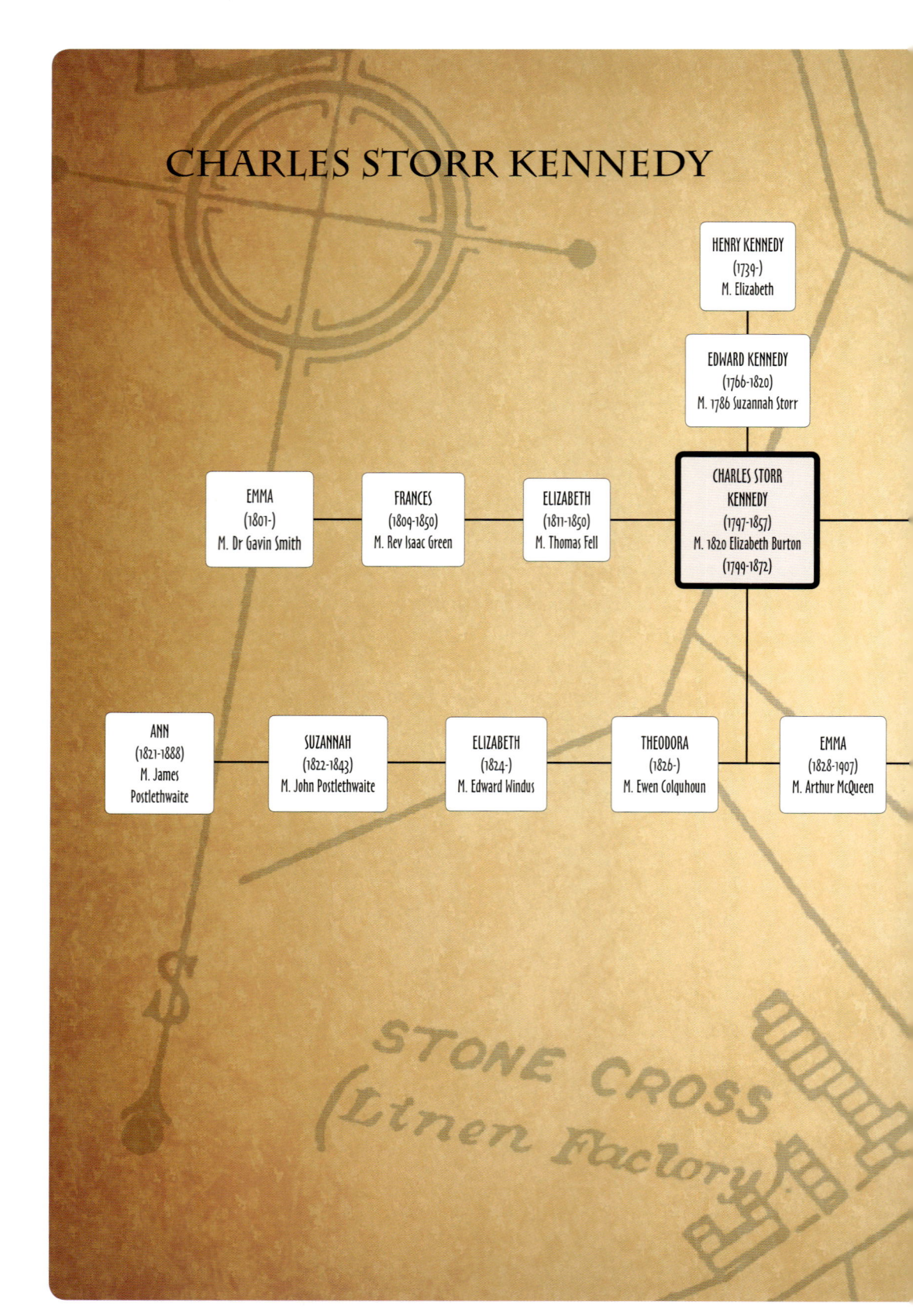

CHARLES STORR KENNEDY

HENRY KENNEDY
(1739-)
M. Elizabeth

EDWARD KENNEDY
(1766-1820)
M. 1786 Suzannah Storr

EMMA
(1801-)
M. Dr Gavin Smith

FRANCES
(1809-1850)
M. Rev Isaac Green

ELIZABETH
(1811-1850)
M. Thomas Fell

CHARLES STORR KENNEDY
(1797-1857)
M. 1820 Elizabeth Burton
(1799-1872)

ANN
(1821-1888)
M. James Postlethwaite

SUZANNAH
(1822-1843)
M. John Postlethwaite

ELIZABETH
(1824-)
M. Edward Windus

THEODORA
(1826-)
M. Ewen Colquhoun

EMMA
(1828-1907)
M. Arthur McQueen

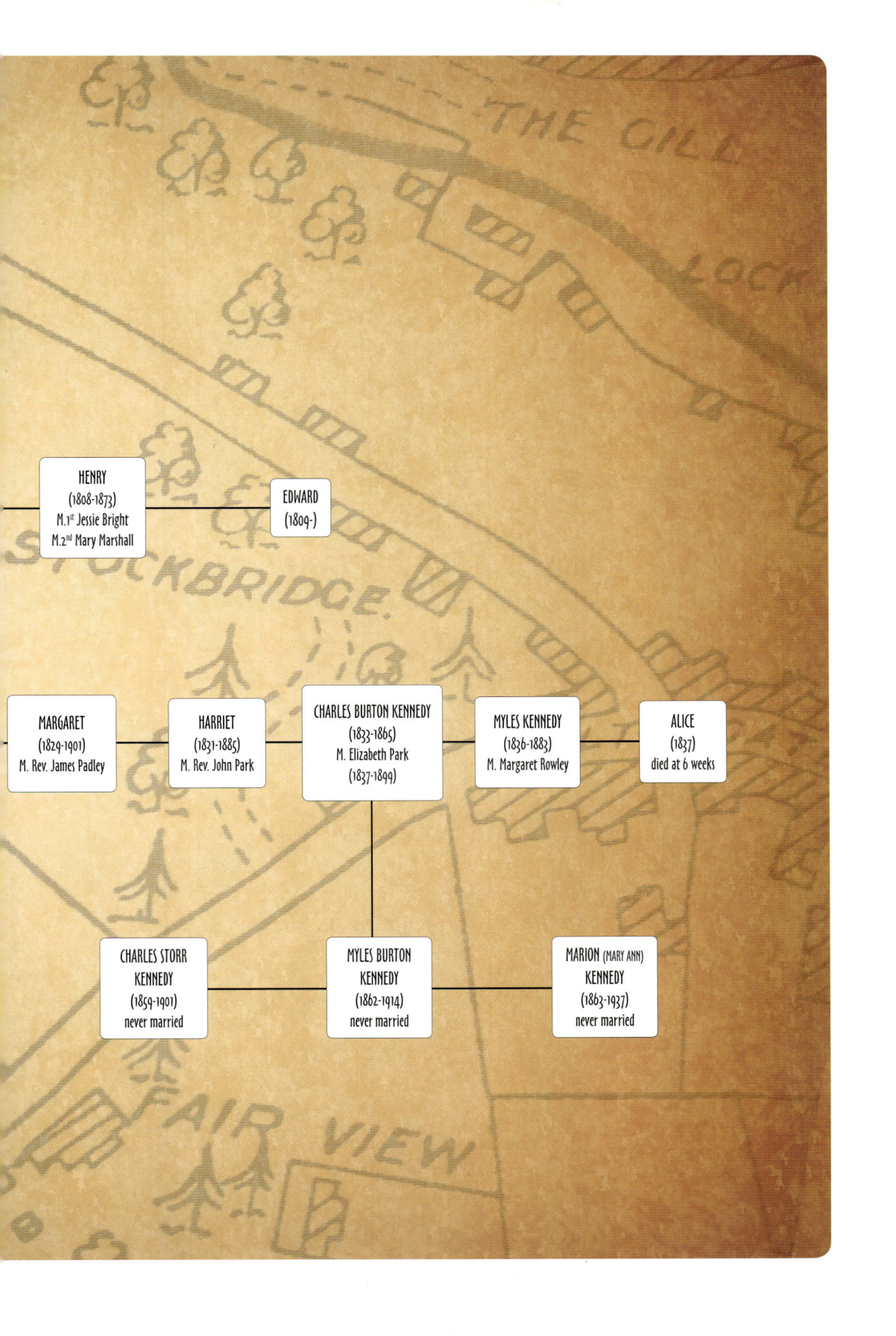

HENRY
(1808-1873)
M.1st Jessie Bright
M.2nd Mary Marshall

EDWARD
(1809-)

MARGARET
(1829-1901)
M. Rev. James Padley

HARRIET
(1831-1885)
M. Rev. John Park

CHARLES BURTON KENNEDY
(1833-1865)
M. Elizabeth Park
(1837-1899)

MYLES KENNEDY
(1836-1883)
M. Margaret Rowley

ALICE
(1837)
died at 6 weeks

CHARLES STORR KENNEDY
(1859-1901)
never married

MYLES BURTON KENNEDY
(1862-1914)
never married

MARION (MARY ANN) KENNEDY
(1863-1937)
never married

Chapter 1

CHARLES STORR KENNEDY

Born 22nd March 1797 • Died 2nd March 1857 aged 59

Charles Storr Kennedy was born on the 22nd March 1797 in Essex. He married Elizabeth Burton (1797-1872) on the 6th September 1820, who was the only daughter of Myles Burton Esq. of Fair View, Ulverston.

Myles Burton was a wealthy businessman who, along with the Fells, had banking and other business interests which included linen sheds within the grounds of the current Stone Cross. Upon his death Elizabeth and Charles inherited Fair View and her father's estate. In the early days Myles Burton was not happy about his daughter's romance with Charles. He pursued them when they tried to elope, brought her back to Ulverston and kept her chaperoned, as noted in a diary belonging to the Dickinson family in 1818 – he must have relented at some point as they were later married and had ten children.

Anne (1821-1881) – m.1840 James Postlethwaite

Suzannah Maria (1822-1843) m. 1840 John Postlethwaite. She died at sea and was buried in Australia. *(In an event that was to be repeated later, two brothers married two sisters)*

Elizabeth (1824) – m. Edward Windus.

Theodora (1826) – m. Ewen Colquhoun. (she wrote the novel 'Farnorth')

Emma (1828-1907) – m. Arthur McQueen.

Margaret (1829-1901) – m. Rev James Padley

Harriet (1831-1885) – m. Rev John Park

Charles Burton Kennedy (1833-1865) m. Elizabeth Park

Myles Kennedy (1836-1883)

Alice (1837-1837) – died 6 weeks old

Charles must have been a visionary for his day as he put in place a sequence of events that would see his immediate descendants earn a vast fortune from Iron Ore.

He began to be involved in prospecting, and engineered the career's of his sons to strengthen the family business. The eldest son, Charles Burton Kennedy entered the legal profession with a view to tying up contracts and his youngest son, Myles, was sent to the Royal School of Mines in preparation of forming a mining company to extract iron ore from the Furness area. After some small successes they hit upon a potentially rich vein at Roanhead.

Unfortunately fate took a turn with a scenario that was to be repeated in the future when Charles died suddenly at Fair View in 1857 aged 60.

The two brothers then had to make a decision – do they trust their father's instinct that Roanhead would prove profitable and press on, risking everything in the process, or not?
Taking the brave decision to continue they struck the equivalent of gold.

They formed Kennedy Brothers and the mines at Roanhead provided them with a fortune.

Elizabeth continued to live at Fair View until her death in 1872. The family also owned Burton Cottage, Kirklands and went on to own Hill Foot which was built around 1853.

On his mother's death, Charles Burton Kennedy took over at Fair View with his wife Elizabeth Park.

During WWI, Fair View was used as a VAD (voluntary aid detachment) hospital for wounded soldiers.

Fair View as it appears today

Chapter 2

THE ROWLEYS

Alexander Butler Rowley was born on the 28th December 1805, the son of the Dean of Lancaster (Joseph Butler Rowley 1780-1864). He married Elizabeth Campbell in Manchester Cathedral on the 13th August 1829. He was a solicitor in the firm Rowley Dickenson and died in 1854. The Rowley family were heavily involved with the formation of Lancashire County Cricket Club. Some of the Rowleys even played for Lancashire with Edmund Rowley being Captain between 1866-79.

They went on to have a large family;

> James Campbell Rowley (1830-1870) – m. Maria Harriet Parkin in 1853
> Joseph Rowley (1832-1908) – m. Annie Clark
> Elizabeth Rowley (1833-) – m. Rev Corbett Moore in 1885
> Margaret Rowley (1834-1887) – m. Myles Kennedy
> Jane Campbell Rowley (1837-1913) – didn't marry
> Alexander Butler Rowley (1837-1911) – m. Hannah Whittaker
> Arthur C Rowley (1840-1862)
> Edmund B Rowley (1842-1905) – m. Lucy Ellen Faulkner
> Walter T Rowley (1844-1924) – m. Eleanor Faulkner
> Septimus Rowley (1846-1874) – m. Emilie
> Alice C Rowley (1848-) – m. John Nelson but divorced and re-married M.R. Matthews

James Campbell Rowley

> Alexander Butler (1857)
> Hugh Campbell (1859)
> Maria Maud (1861)
> Amy Gertrude (1862)
> Arthur Herbert (1863-1887) died in Canada
> Joseph Parkin (1864)

Leonard.   Joseph Rowley.   "Harry Butler

Joseph Rowley... went on to have a large family of his own;

Blanch (1863-1943) m. William Marks

Florence (1864-1939)
m. Arthur Spafford

Ethel Campbell (1866-1943)
m. Myles Kennedy (her cousin)

Annie Maud (1867-1948)
m. Roger Strickland

Alice Campbell (1868-1958)
m. Theobald Kennedy (cousin)

Edith May (1873-1952)
m. T Kemply Irwin

Harry Butler (1875-1929)
m. Henrietta Strickland

Emilie Brenda (1877-1931) never married and died in a special hospital (left £2,000 in her will to Alice Campbell)

Joseph A Leonard (1880-1910)

Ursula Gladys (1887)

Joseph Rowley with his daughter Ethel

Edmund B Rowley

Widowed by 1881 and left £11,862 to his son Ernest.

Ernest (1870-1962) – m. Minnie Keyworth.
Mabel Campbell Rowley (1871-1969) – m. Captain Lionel Frederic Leader in 1897. LFL died in Canada in 1939.

Ernest Rowley
Ethel Kennedy
Hugh Kennedy

Toboganning
December 1906 (xmas week)

Walter T Rowley

Mildred (1871)
Theobald (1873)
Dora Campbell (1875-1952)
Married her cousin Alfred Kennedy
Douglas (1882)
Charles (1888)
Gerald (1895)

Back row Left to right
Dora Kennedy, Major Alfred Kennedy, Ethel Kennedy, Flo Spafford.

Front row Left to right
Mr Hart Jackson, Mr Holbin, Ethel M Kennedy, Mylie Kennedy, Sybil G B Kennedy, Myles Burton Kennedy.

Alexander Butler Rowley

Oldham Whittaker (1865-1952) – m. Evelyn Drury

Helen Elizabeth (1866-1919) – m. *Ernest Henry Ainslie.

Ernest Henry Ainslie's father, Henry, was a vicar. His father was Montague Ainslie who married Agnes Ford. They inherited the Grizedale Estate via Agnes and had Ford House built in Ford Park, Ulverston. The Kennedys went on to have a long relationship with the Ainslie family with W.G.A. Kennedy being named after Montague's son, William George Ainslie. Unfortunately Helen and Ernest's marriage was not successful which resulted in a very, public divorce which saw the Grizedale estate being sold to the Brocklebanks in 1903 who re-built the Hall. Another one of Montague's children, Mary, married the local agent, Edward Wadham who was very influential in all the Furness industries.

Alice Blanche C (1868-1956) – never married and was an artist.

Edith Campbell (1870-1947) – m. Major Willoughby Gwatkin (later to become a Sir). Unfortunately this marriage also resulted in divorce in 1896 when Edith was proved to have committed adultery with Charles Waterer and being with child. She later m. Charles and they went on to have more children together.

Constance Mable (1872-1952) – m. Ralph Henderson.

Alexander Butler (1874-1946) – m. Gladys Read (A.B.R. was at Harrow at the same time as Winston Churchill).

Walter and Mylie Kennedy with their Father and Mother-in-Law

Chapter 3

CHARLES BURTON KENNEDY

Born 1833 • Died 1865 Aged 31

Charles Burton Kennedy married Elizabeth Park. They had three children. First, Charles Storr Kennedy (born 11th October 1859), followed by their second son Myles Burton Kennedy (born 30th December 1862) and finally a daughter, Marion (born 15th September 1863). None of them married or had children and are interred in Holy Trinity Churchyard, Ulverston. Their family home was Fair View and they also had a residence at 118 Piccadilly London where in the 1901 census they had seven servants living in.

118 Picadilly today

Again tragedy struck and Charles Burton Kennedy died in 1865 aged 31. A legal battle ensued in what was to become 'Kennedy versus Kennedy' which involved his wife Elizabeth Park who later remarried a solicitor named Frank Scargil. Charles Burton Kennedy left his estate to his brother in trust for his sons and when Myles died in 1883 at the age of 47, he left Fair View to Charles Storr Kennedy.

Charles Storr Kennedy

Charles Storr Kennedy died 9th May 1901 at the early age of 41. He left his collection of over 100 Battersea enamels to his brother who later donated them to the Victoria & Albert Museum.

Myles Burton Kennedy went on to become a renowned yachtsman, who competed in many races, including against the Kaiser at Cowes in the early 1900's. He had great success particularly with White Heather II with which in 1913 he won the King's Cup for the fourth time. He was a member of the Royal Yacht Squadron, the Royal Automobile Club and when he died on the 12th June 1914 aged 51, his estate was valued at over £250,000 (over £20 million today).

Myles Burton Kennedy left his real estate in Lancashire to Nigel Kennedy along with £500 a year, his gold trophies and jewellery to his sister Marion and an assortment of items and monies to friends and former staff.

Myles Burton Kennedy

10

On board White Heather II
Roger Strickland, Commander Kennedy, Maude Strickland

Lord Nelson day 1906

Lord Nelson Day was celebrated on 21st October. It is sometimes referred to as Trafalgar Day in celebration of Nelson's victory over the French and Spanish fleets in 1805. As the Kennedys were a Naval family, they appeared to take great pride in this celebration as seen here.

Myles Burton Kennedy bottom left on staircase at Stone Cross

Chapter 4

MYLES KENNEDY

Born 9th February 1836 • Died 13th March 1883 aged 47

Myles Kennedy was born at Fair View on the 9th February 1836 as the second son. He married Margaret Rowley at Manchester Cathedral in 1861. The Rowleys were a large family who were to be intertwined with the Kennedys further later on. They lived at Hill Foot and after Myles decided not to pursue the purchase of Conishead Priory, had Stone Cross Mansion built in 1874 taking approximately 5 years to complete. They went on to have 16 children.

Myles was a great asset to the town of Ulverston being at the forefront of all good causes. He was the Captain Commandant of the Ulverston Volunteer Corps, Chairman of the Local Board, a large subscriber of the Cottage Hospital (donating the Land on which it was to be built), Principal Patron of the Music and Dramatic performances, Local Magistrate and an active Freemason who enjoyed the role of Country Gentleman having an open breakfast at Stone Cross at his New Year Hunt.

Then, in what was becoming a repeating tragedy, Myles died suddenly at Stone Cross on 13th March 1883, he was only 47 years old. Upon his death his estate was valued at £276,000 (around £27 million by today's standards).

In his will he left Fair View to his nephew, Charles Storr Kennedy. To his wife he left his wines, consumable stores, jewellery, horses and carriages. The residue of his real and personal estate was to be held in trust for his wife to receive rents, dividends and income for the rest of her life or until she married again, then pass to his children with the eldest son to receive five times as much as each of his other sons with each son receiving twice as much as each daughter.

THE LATE MYLES KENNEDY.

After Margaret's death in 1887 Stone Cross and its furnishings were put up for sale in 1888.

Stone Cross Mansion in its heyday

South face

Coach house yard

Courtyard

North face
rose garden

Ethel in the Rose Garden
(The rose garden would have been a tranquil place but in later years, when transformed into a school most of this area was lost to building extensions and alterations)

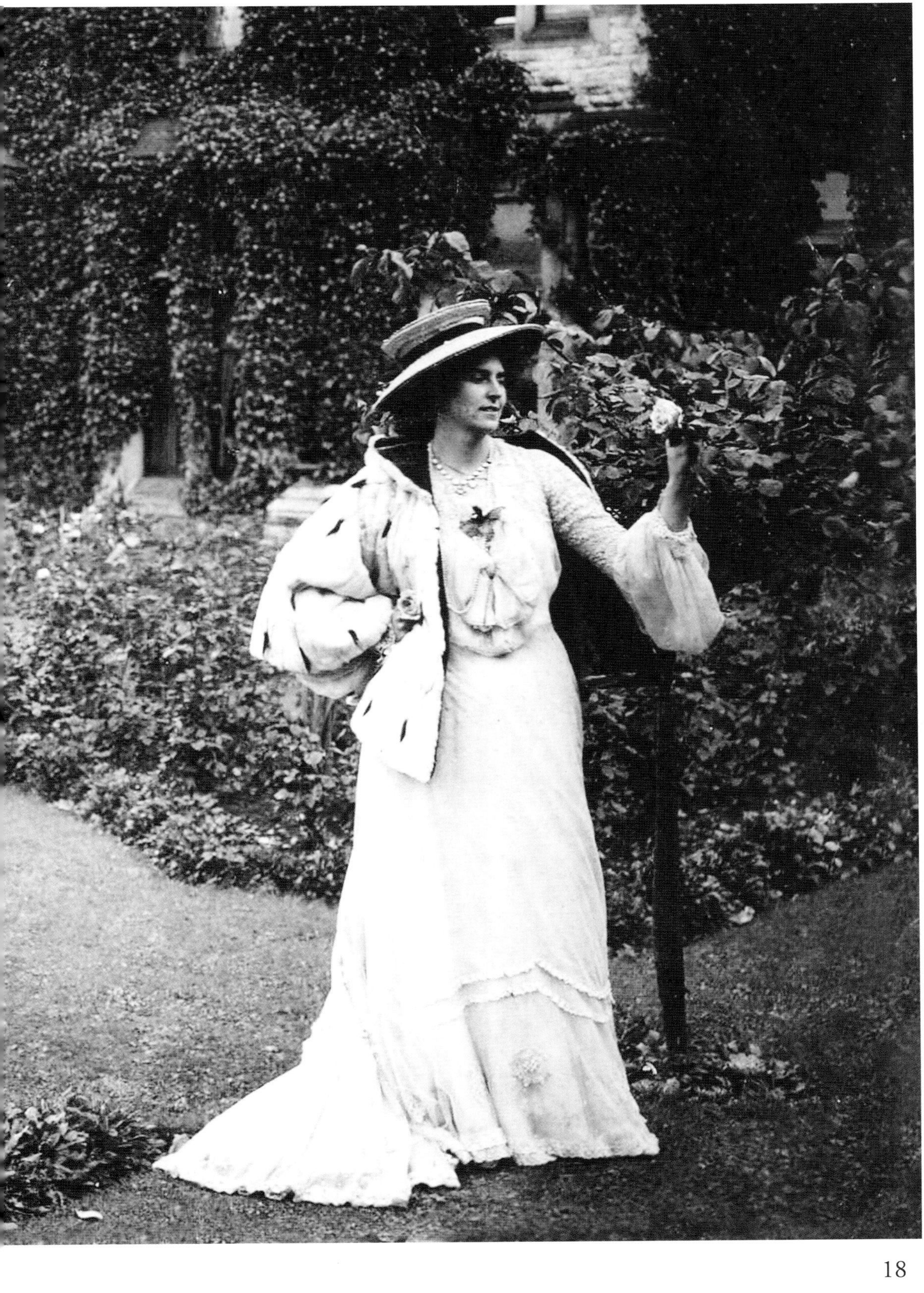

Myles Kennedy - a summary.

Born on the 9th February 1836 – the youngest son of 10 children to Charles Storr Kennedy. With his brother Charles Burton Kennedy formed Kennedy Brothers and took over their fathers' mining prospects. He married Margaret Rowley and produced 16 children shown here in a family portrait.

Over the next few chapters we will examine the lives of these children as they experienced one of the most turbulent times in modern history.

HENRY KENNEDY (1734-) M. Elizabeth

EDWARD KENNEDY (1760-1820) M. Suzannah Storr

CHARLES STORR KENNEDY (1797-1867) M. Elizabeth Burton

MYLES KENNEDY (1836-1883) M. (1860) Margaret Rowley (1835-1887)

1862 Myles Theodore Burton (03/06/1862. Aged 20 when his father died)
1863 Wilfred Burton Rowley (18/07/1863. Aged 19 when his father died)
1864 Marguerite Rowley (09/1864. Aged 18 when her father died)
1865 Alice Storr (24/10/1865. Aged 17 when her father died)
1866 Elizabeth Burton (06/10/1866. Aged 16 when her father died)
1867 Florence Campbell (05/10/1867. Aged 15 when her father died)
1868 Kathleen (03/11/1868. Aged 14 when her father died)
1869 Mary Maud (24/11/1869. Aged 13 when her father died)
1870 Alfred Alexander (10/12/1870. Aged 12 when his father died)
1871 Theobald Walter Butler (12/12/1871. Aged 11 when his father died)
1872 Violet (12/1872. Aged 10 when her father died)
1873 William George Ainslie (16/09/1873. Aged 9 when his father died)
1874 Started Stone Cross
1874 Lucy (18/08/1874. Born and died when her father was aged 38)
1875 Emma (03/09/1875. Aged 7 when her father died)
1876 Mabel (09/1876. Aged 6 when her father died)
1877 Arthur Herbert (27/10/1877. Aged 5 when his father died)
1879 Finished Stone Cross
1883 Died 13/03

MYLES (1862-1928) M. Ethel Rowley

WILFRED (1863-1894) M. Emelia Strenger

MARGUERITE (1864-1930) M. Henry Wilson

ALICE (1865-1851) M. Henry Lewis

ELIZABETH (1866-1961) M. Ellliksen & H White

FLORENCE (1867-1948) M. Charles Fisher

KATHLEEN (1868-1950) M. Henry Trollope

MARY (1869-1926) M. Myles Trollope

ALFRED (1870-1926) M. Dora Rowley

T WALTER (1871-1934) M. Alice Rowley

VIOLET (1872-1956) M. William Tower

WILLIAM (1873-1938) M. Alice Lundh

LUCY (1874)

EMMA (1875-1951) never married

MABEL (1876-1954) M. Geoffrey Hopwood

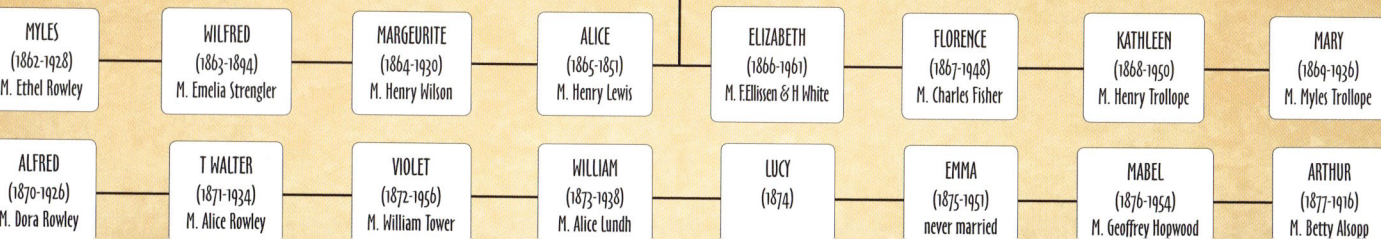

ARTHUR (1877-1916) M. Betty Alsopp

ELIZABETH
WILFRED
MARY MAUDE
MARGUERITE
ALFRED
MARGARET
MABEL
ALICE
VIOLET
KATHLEEN
MYLES
EMMA
WILLIAM
MYLIE
T.WALTER
FLORENCE

Chapter 5

MYLES THEODORE BURTON KENNEDY

Born 3rd June 1862 • Died 9th August 1928 aged 66

Myles Theodore Burton Kennedy was born 3rd June 1862 as the eldest child of Myles and Margaret (née Rowley) and was also referred to as Mylie. During his early years he was raised at Hill Foot and went on to be educated

MYLES KENNEDY
(1836-1883)
M. 1860 Margaret
Rowley (1835-1887)

MYLES
(1862-1928)
M. 1885 Ethel
Rowley (1966-1943)

THEODORE	MYLES STORR NIGEL KENNEDY	WILFRED H. BURTON	ETHEL MARGUERITE	SYBIL GUINIVERE BUTLER
1885	1889-1964	1893-1971	1886-1941	1890-1973
	m. Dorothy Millington	m. Violet Wilson	m. Herbert Goldsmith Squires	m. James Ogilvy-Dalgleish
	(no children)	(2 children)	(3 children)	(2 children)

at Harrow, in the same year as Bruce Ismay of Titanic fame, and later went to The Royal School of mines.

As the family had a strong connection with London they often spent a lot of time there, indeed on the 1881 census, when he was 18, he was living at 126 & 127 Bond Street with his father, mother, brother Wilfred and sister Elizabeth whilst another sister, Alice, stayed at home looking after Stone Cross and her remaining siblings.

He was 20 years old when his father died and he married his first cousin Ethel Campbell Rowley, who was the daughter of his mother's brother. They were married at Manchester Cathedral on 10th February 1885. On what was probably their honeymoon in America, they sat for portraits at Taber's studios on Montgomery Street, San Francisco. Isaiah West Taber was already becoming a respected photographer who was later commissioned for portraits of the soon to be Edward VII. Unfortunately the 1906 San Francisco earthquake destroyed his studio and negatives

Ethel was born in 1866 and was one of 10 children born to

Joseph (born 1832 – died 18/11/1908) and Annie Rowley. Another daughter, and sister of Ethel, Alice Campbell Rowley married Myles's brother Theobald Walter Butler Kennedy and another cousin of theirs, Dora Campbell Rowley married another brother Alfred Alexander Kennedy.

Myles took over the family mantle with tremendous endeavour and was prominent in most of the good causes of the town and district. He became a JP, High Sheriff, was influential in the formation of Ulverston Golf Club, laid the foundation stone for the Coronation Hall and the Masonic Lodge as well as being a Patron of Grasmere Sports.

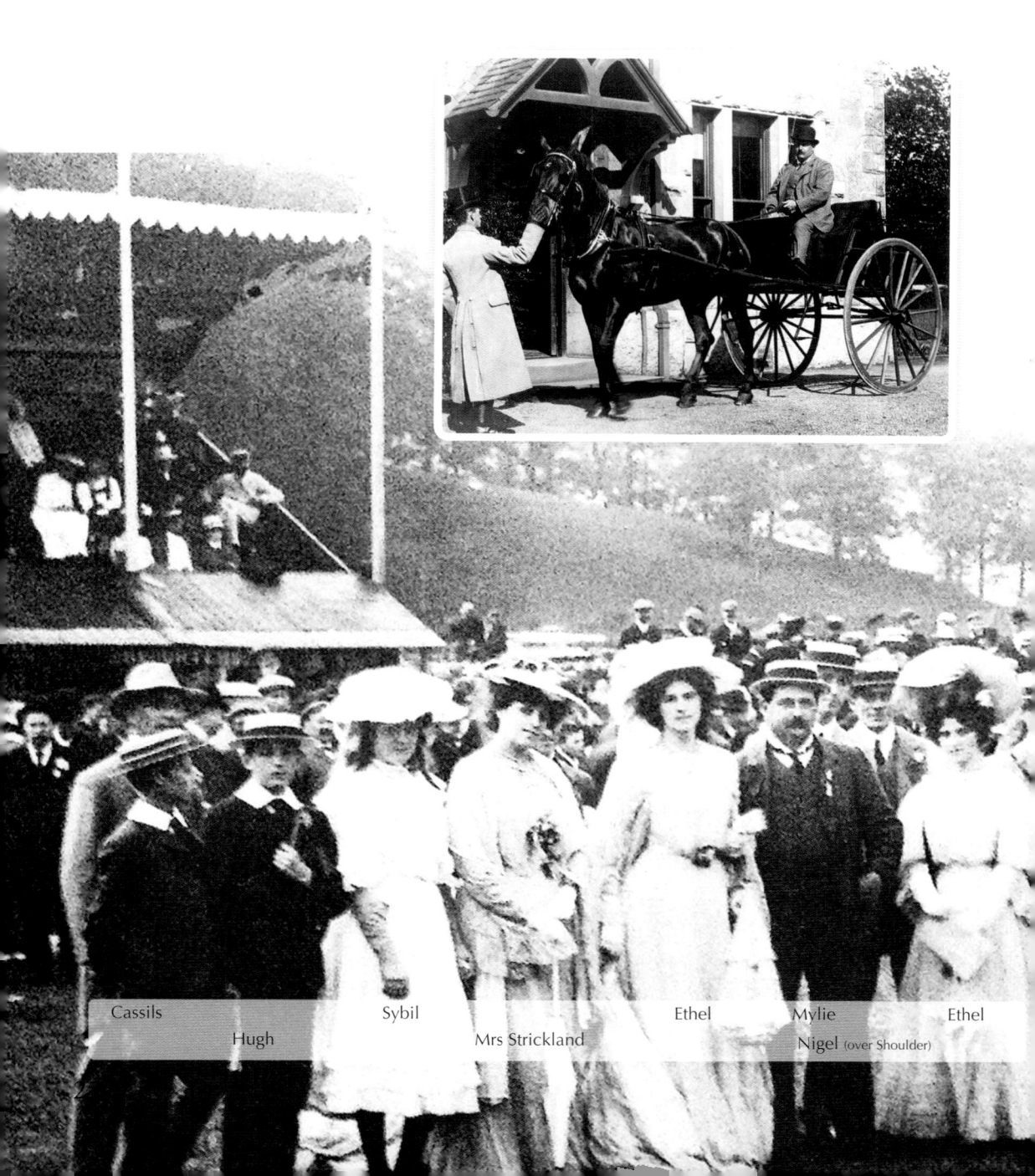

| Cassils | | Sybil | | Ethel | Mylie | Ethel |
| Hugh | | | Mrs Strickland | | Nigel (over shoulder) | |

Myles and Ethel first had a son called Theodore who was born 19/9/1885 but died prematurely the following day. They went on to have four more children.

When he died on 9th August 1928 he left an estate valued at £100,000. Ethel died in 1943.

Earl of Lonsdale

Grasmere Sports Early 1900's

Thomas Newby Wilson

Myles Storr Nigel Kennedy

Born 12th October 1889 and went on to be educated at Harrow and Trinity College Cambridge.

Myles was known locally as Nigel and served as a Captain in WWI with the 3rd Borders, he fought in the first battle of Ypres. He was mentioned twice in despatches and wounded on 19th December 1914.

He went on to become a Major and carried on the family interests at Ulverston Golf Club where they still play for the Kennedy Cup.

He served as an MP for the Conservative Party in the 1922 election.

He continued the family mining business at Roanhead and was later a member of Lancashire County Council. Unfortunately he was declared

Nigel No.1 Pit. Roanhead Hematite Iron Mines

bankrupt in 1941 for the sum of £2,000 owing to an action brought by a Miss Marie Harrison for breach of promise. She was a head bar maid at the Grand Hotel Leicester and resisted his original advances until a visit to her Mother's house led to the announcement of an engagement and celebration at the hotel when he gave her a diamond ring and later a car. Although Myles did not seem to take the engagement seriously as when she confronted him about when their proposed marriage was due to take place, he is reported to have said it was nothing he 'couldn't get out of' but the judge sided with Miss Harrison.

Later in life he resided at Hill Foot where at one point he was known to have 28 dogs with his wife Dorothy Millington, the only daughter of John Millington of Leicester who he married on the 18th July 1946. They had no children and Myles died in 1964.

Wilfred Hugh Burton Rowley Kennedy

Born 2nd November 1893 and was educated at Harrow. He went on to become High Sheriff of Lancashire in 1949 and retired a Colonel after serving with the Home Guard.

He served as a JP and lived at Fair View before moving away.

On the 29th April 1919 he married Violet Enid Wilson who was awarded an OBE for services to nursing during WWI.

Violet's mother was called Florence Wilson (her maiden name Cammell from the Cammell Laird shipping fame). She was murdered whilst walking home from Le Touquet Golf course in France and the killer or killers where never caught.

Violet

During WWI he served as a Lieutenant with the 4th Kings Own Royal Lancashire Regiment and was wounded in July 1917.

Hugh also had a brush with a personal tragedy in 1928 when he was playing the mess game of 'flying somersaults' at a regimental dinner at the Park Hotel Preston. The game involves two players, the first bends down and puts his hands through his legs. The second then grasps his companion's wrists and, lifting the player from the ground causes him to turn a somersault and land on his feet. Col. Kennedy, being the officer who was going to lift the player with his hands between his legs, first asked if Lt Col F.W. Baker Young was ready and to confirm that his hands weren't crossed to which Col. Young confirmed that they weren't. He must have had his hands crossed as Col. Kennedy could not hold him. Col. Young lost his grip which caused him to crack his head on the concrete floor and die. The inquest cleared Hugh of any blame but it must have been a heavy burden to live with knowing a simple high jinks game had resulted in his comrade's death. Frederic William Baker Young was a GP until after the war when he gradually relinquished his practice and became a specialist in dermatology. Col. Young was married but had no children and was given a full military funeral, he was aged 49.

Hugh also carried on the family interest at Ulverston Golf Club and died in 1971.

They had two sons, firstly, Anthony Myles Hugh Kennedy who was born 16th January 1921. Anthony served as a Captain with the Staff. Yeom. in WWII where he received the Military Cross. In 1944 the then Lt. Kennedy was interviewed as a tank officer by the Evening Telegraph on the 1st July. He commended his men, reporting that although most of them were under 21 years of age they fought courageously through the Normandy Wood which was to become known as 'Suicide Wood'. Lt. Kennedy described the experience as absolute hell compared with the desert fighting he was use to due to 'Jerry's strong resolve' and the anti-tank guns. Both sides knew the strategic importance of this wood and it was a glorious achievement by the Regiment to overcome the enemy. He too studied at Harrow.

After the war he settled in Rhodesia where on the 17th March 1951 he married Irene Frost from South Africa. They went on to have three children. The second son was Michael Herbert Rowley Kennedy who was a market gardener. He served with the Home Guard in WWII between 1940-1946, combined with a spell in the RAF. He was born 14th March 1923 and lived at Kirklands. He was educated at Badingham College.

His first wife was Audrey Jenni Cooper who he married on the 30th March 1949 and had an adopted daughter called Georgina Elizabeth but he and Audrey divorced and he married Jean Dunkerly of Ulverston on 22nd May 1957.

They had a son Myles Kennedy who currently resides in Ulverston, South Cumbria.

Ethel Marguerite Kennedy

The eldest daughter and was born on the 17th November 1886. She was known in the family as 'Snowball'.

She was presented at a debutants ball at Buckingham Palace on Friday 13th May 1904 in the company of the King and Queen, Prince and Princess of Wales and other members of the Royal Family with Princess Victoria of Connaught also being presented. The function was held in the throne room and was reportedly very impressive. Marguerite, along with her Mother, must have made an impression as they were named in the press as being present and their dresses described in detail. It just goes to show the circles they must have been moving in, maybe some connections were made via Myles's cousin, Myles Burton Kennedy, the famous yachtsman as he was a member of the Royal Yacht and Automobile clubs.

Ethel married Herbert Goldsmith Squires Jnr on 2nd February 1916. HGS Jnr was the son of the well known American Diplomat Herbert Goldsmith Squires Snr who during his time served as Minister to Cuba and Panama. HGS Jnr died due to a scalding incident on the 29th September 1941 aged 49 in Nairobi, Kenya.

Ethel died at Aratoma Lodge, Gilgil, Kenya on the 28th January 1949 after a long illness, she was 62 years old.

With their American and Diplomatic connections, they appeared to do a lot of travelling.

They had 3 sons, Herbert Goldsmith Squires who was born in 26/06/1917.

Myles Christian Campbell Squires who was born in 1923 and who served as a sergeant in the RAF in WWII with 102 Squadron on a Halifax known as G-George as Air Gunner. In a tragic flight he was to lose his life. Stationed at Polkington on the 29th March 1943, it was a cloudy, icy Monday night and whilst in the process of setting off on an evening bomb-

Sgt. Myles Squiers | F/O Douglas Harper | F/S Bill Comrie | Sgt. Frank Dorrington | P/O William Jenkins

ing mission to Germany it is reported that the pilot, Flight Sgt. Bill Comrie, whilst seen as a first class pilot, had to take evasive action to avoid another aircraft. Afterwards it was suggested, that a late decision to go ahead with missions due to the inclement weather meant that too many aircraft were airborne at once. The pilot managed to steer the plane away from the town but could not recover the aircraft which crashed into West Green, killing all the crew.

Myles was engaged to Stella Thomas of Ulverston and they had plans to marry and go to South Africa after the war. Myles was aged 20 when he died and is buried at Barmby-on-The-Moor Churchyard of St Catherine's Yorkshire. The families of those lost were given the choice of where the burials would take place.

The third son was called Arthur Butler Squires and was born on the 11th February 1924.

On the 26th March 1946 he married Louise Gabrielle Humphrys, youngest daughter of Captain Hugh Everard Humphrys of Honington House, Suffolk

He died in Workingham Berks in December 1996 aged 72.

Sybil Guinivere Butler Kennedy

Born on the 11th December 1890 and was known in the family as Baba.

She was originally engaged to Capt. Mervyn Keats Sandys whose family where from Graythwaite Hall. Mervyn was the younger of twins born 17th July 1864, his twin George Owen Sandys later inheriting Graythwaite Hall. They announced their intended engagement in January 1914.

In WWI Mervyn was serving with the 2nd York & Lancaster's but was killed in action around 23rd October 1914. Although there is a memorial at Hainaut, they never recovered his body. In 2006 a soldier's body was recovered and it was suggested he was an officer from this regiment. Mervyn was one two possible officers unaccounted for in this location but no formal identification has been made and the soldier's body has now been laid to rest.

Sybil was also presented at a debutants ball and is seen here as a bridesmaid.

On the 28th June 1916, a Wednesday, which seemed to be the fashionable day to marry in those times, Sybil married Flt Comm. James William Ogilvy-Dalgleish. He was from a very well-known Fifeshire family with a strong military and naval history.

In May 1915 an airship passed over Stone Cross, en-route to Barrow which was later discovered to be under the command of James, it was named 'Silver Queen'. James ended up a Wing Comm. and received an OBE in the 1940's and was also High Sheriff of Rutland. He died in 1969 aged 83.

Sybil died in Edgecombe Nursing Home Newbury on 22nd March 1973 aged 82.

They had 2 daughters, Joan who was born 21st March 1917. She married Richard Margery Hole of RNVR on 9th April 1947 at St Saviours Church, Chelsea and they had children. Joan died 3rd April 2012 aged 95, Richard died in 1995.

Their other daughter was named Elizabeth who married John Norman on the 4th October 1968.

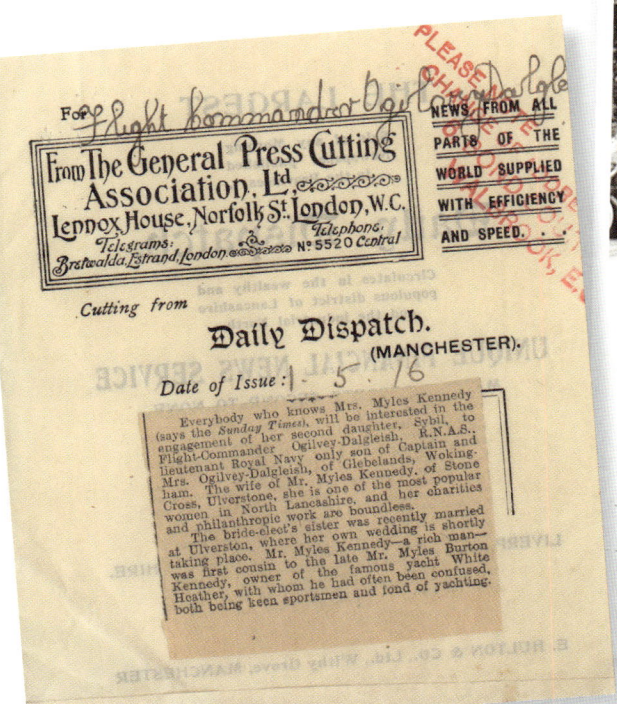

From The General Press Cutting Association, Ltd
Lennox House, Norfolk St, London, W.C.
Telegrams: Britwalda, Estrand, London.
Telephone N° 5520 Central

Cutting from **Daily Dispatch.** (MANCHESTER).

Date of Issue: 1.5.16

Everybody who knows Mrs. Myles Kennedy (says the *Sunday Times*), will be interested in the engagement of her second daughter, Sybil, to Flight-Commander Ogilvey-Dalgleish, R.N.A.S., Lieutenant Royal Navy only son of Captain and Mrs. Ogilvey-Dalgleish, of Glebelands, Wokingham. The wife of Mr. Myles Kennedy, of Stone Cross, Ulverstone, she is one of the most popular women in North Lancashire, and her charities and philanthropic work are boundless.
The bride-elect's sister was recently married at Ulverston, where her own wedding is shortly taking place. Mr. Myles Kennedy—a rich man—was first cousin to the late Mr. Myles Burton Kennedy, owner of the famous yacht White Heather, with whom he had often been confused, both being keen sportsmen and fond of yachting.

The Wedding of Sybil and Flt Comm. James William Ogilvy-Dalgleish.

Wednesday 28th June 1916

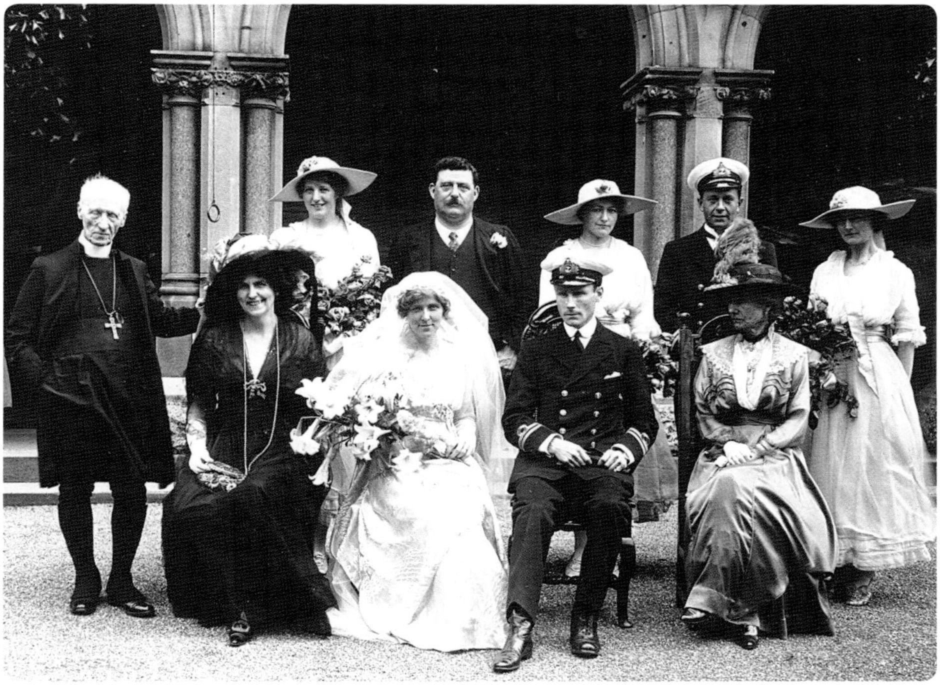

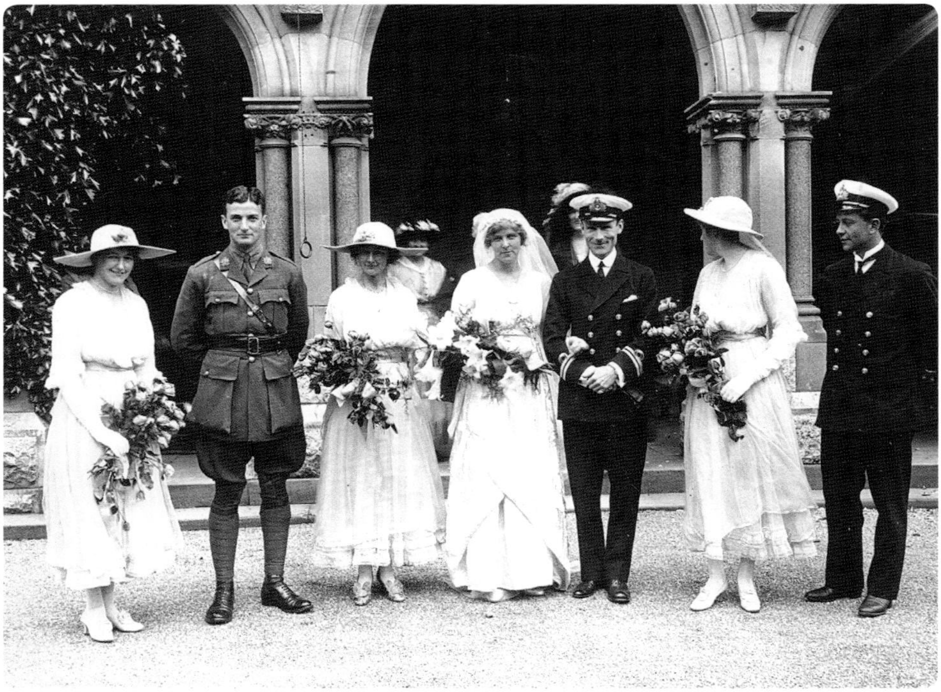

Chapter 6

WILFRED BURTON ROWLEY KENNEDY

Born 18th July 1863 • Died 18th August 1894 Aged 31

Wilfred Burton Rowley Kennedy was born on the 18th July 1863. His middle names came from his mother and grandmother's maiden names. He was only 19 when his father died.

Wilfred studied at Trinity Hall, Cambridge. He became a Lieutenant in the 1st Volunteer Battalion of The King's Own Royal Lancashire Regiment in 1888 and was later promoted to Colonel in the 4th Battalion of the Royal Lancashire Regiment. In early 1886 a marriage was arranged between Wilfred and Miss Marianne S E Peyton who was the eldest daughter of J E H Peyton but there is no record of the marriage actually taking place and she married someone else several years later.

In 1887 he married Emielie Augusta Stengler and settled in Norway. He lived life there as a country gent and bought a match factory along with a house he named Ulverston. On the 10th September 1893 they had a son Myles Cassils Kennedy but before his son was one year old, Wilfred died tragically aged only 31. It was rumoured that his death was linked to morphine and depression.

His elder brother Myles took his wife, young child and maid back to Stone Cross but the maid couldn't settle and returned to Norway. Emielie had little grasp of English and struggled adjusting to life in England. When trying to resolve issues with Wilfred's will, his brother Myles described her as, 'childlike in many ways' and had to manage his brother's estate on her behalf. As with other family members, they held shares in Kennedy Bros. so an allowance was given to her to live on via any dividends paid out. She died in Droitwitch on the 27th November 1902.

MYLES KENNEDY
(1836-1883)
M. 1860 Margaret Rowley (1835-1887)

WILFRED
(1863-1894)
M. 1887 Emielie Stengler

MYLES CASSILS
(1893-1947)
M. 1st 1917 Beryl Gossling
M. 2nd 1933 Molly Pady

Myles Cassils

was brought up with his cousins at Stone Cross and went on to become a Captain in the 3rd Hussars and was mentioned in despatches in WWI. His Uncle Myles had to write a letter to allow him to join the army stating that he was his brother's son and a British Citizen.

He married firstly Beryl Gossling on 15th November 1917 in Chelsea and they had two daughters, Zoe Nadine born in 1919 but she died in 1925 and Valerie Susan born 28th February 1921 and died in November 1995. She married a Major Roderick Edward Norris (born 2/8/1920 in Argentina – died 13th Feb 1998 in Sussex) on the 3rd April 1944 and they 2 daughters.

In 1933 he married Molly Mildred Pady and had a further two daughters. Jacqueline was born 17th February 1933 but died after 2 operations on 1st June 1936 after swallowing a coin. Diana Elizabeth was born 27th December 1935 and went to marry a Belgian, John Morel on the 14th March 1959 and they went on to have children of their own.

Chapter 7

MARGUERITE ROWLEY KENNEDY MBE

Born September 1864 • Died 17th August 1930 Aged 65
Married Name Wilson

Marguerite Rowley Kennedy was born in September 1864 and was 18 when her father died. She is recorded in the 1881 census as a pupil in residence at 106 Lansdowne Place, Hove, Sussex when she was 16.

In August 1888 she married Henry C Wilson who later went on to become a Major.

In the 1891 census she was living at Langley House Hastings with her husband and two young children. At the same time it appears they must have taken in some of her siblings after her father's death as her sisters Elizabeth aged 24, Mary aged 23 and youngest brother Arthur aged 13 were all living with her.

By 1901 they had 11 servants and more of their own children;

Marjorie Violet Wilson (1889-) m.George Henry Buley (1885-1939)

Harry John Malcolm Wilson (1890-) A Captain seconded to the New Zealand Expedition Force.

Dorothy Maud Wilson (1892-) m.Francis Henry Moore Trollope. (Francis was the nephew of John Evelyn and Henry Charles Trollope who married Marguerite's sisters). On his death in 1946 his estate was valued at £ 12,727.

Marguerite Louisa Wilson (1894-)

Kate Daphne Wilson (1895-1977) m.Fred Stafford Hodge (1891-)

Percy Frederick Wilson (1897-1977) m.Winifred N Gibbons (1905-1957) and died in NZ

Florence Esme Wilson (1899)

Arthur Cecil Wilson (1900-1975) m.Margaret B Lliffe (1908-1993) and had a son George Robin Wilson.

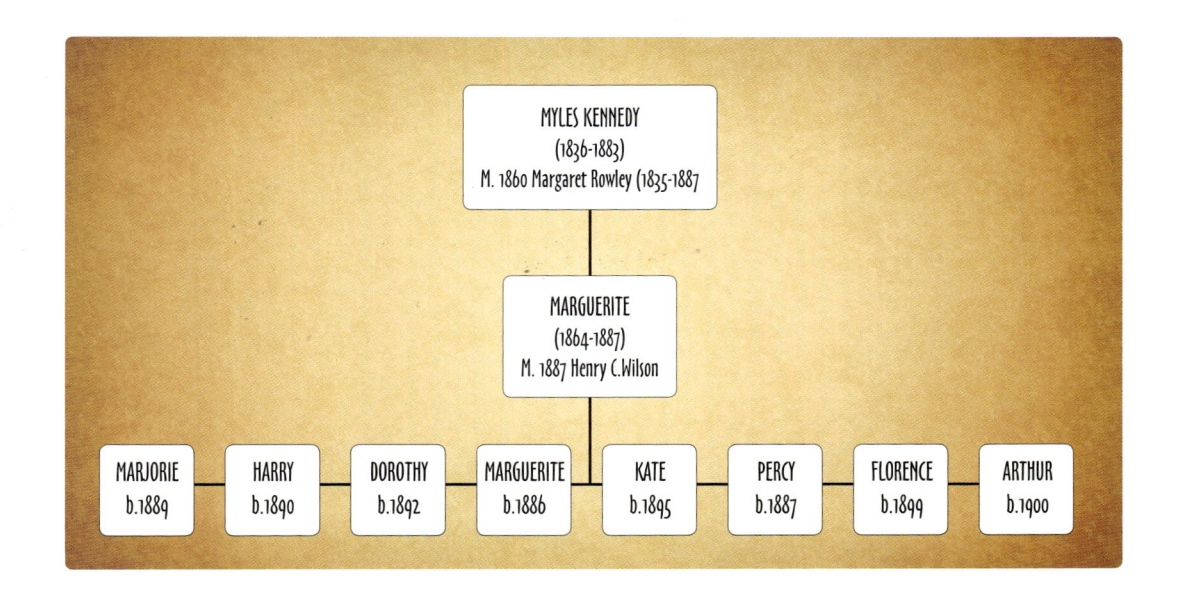

```
                        MYLES KENNEDY
                         (1836-1883)
              M. 1860 Margaret Rowley (1835-1887)
                              |
                         MARGUERITE
                         (1864-1887)
                    M. 1887 Henry C. Wilson
                              |
  ┌─────────┬─────────┬─────────┬─────────┬─────────┬─────────┬─────────┐
MARJORIE  HARRY   DOROTHY MARGUERITE KATE    PERCY  FLORENCE  ARTHUR
b.1889   b.1890   b.1892   b.1886  b.1895  b.1887   b.1899   b.1900
```

By 1911 they were living at Ebury Lodge in Surrey, and later went on to live at Each Manor. They did fall on difficult financial times later.

Marguerite was one of the founding members of the VAD hospital set up in Ash village hall near Sandwich. She was one of the first people in the country to receive the MBE for her nursing work during WWI where she served as Commandant.

Marguerite died on Sunday 17th August 1930 aged 66 in a nursing home in Folkestone leaving her brother Walter as executor of her will amounting to £4747.

Chapter 8
ALICE STORR KENNEDY

Born 29th October 1865 • Died 21st November 1951 Aged 86
Married Name Lewis

Alice Storr Kennedy was born 29th October 1865 and was 17 when her father died.

On the 18th March 1885 she married Lt Henry Francis Peterkin Lewis, (1841-1935) who became a Colonel. In 1881 he was a Major at Bull Point Barracks.

They had two children, a son, **Francis L.K. Lewis** born around 1886 in Hastings.

Their daughter, **Anna M.E. Lewis** was born on 17th November 1887 and died a spinster in 1982.

In the 1881 census Alice, was left as the head of house at Stone Cross whilst her parents were away in London with some of her siblings.

In the 1901 census she was living with Henry & Francis in Cheltenham.

In 1935 Henry Lewis left an estate of £41,624 to his daughter, Anna.

Alice died on the 21st November 1951 aged 86 leaving her estate valued at £ 11,237 also to Anna.

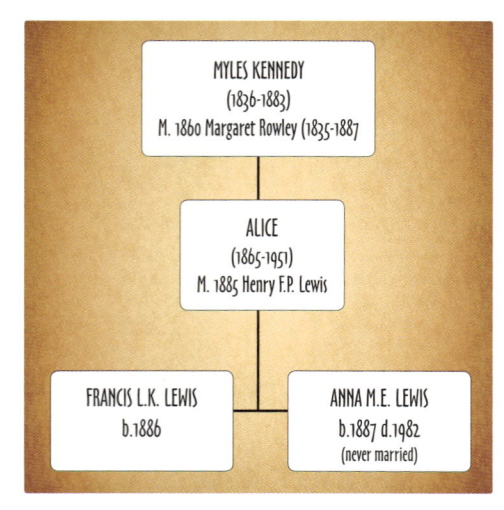

```
MYLES KENNEDY
(1836-1883)
M. 1860 Margaret Rowley (1835-1887)
        |
      ALICE
    (1865-1951)
M. 1885 Henry F.P. Lewis
        |
   ┌────┴────┐
FRANCIS L.K. LEWIS    ANNA M.E. LEWIS
    b.1886            b.1887 d.1982
                      (never married)
```

Alice and Henry Lewis

Chapter 9
ELIZABETH BURTON KENNEDY

Born 6th October 1866 • Died 28th July 1961 Aged 94
Married Names 1st Ellissen, 2nd Wingate-White

Elizabeth Burton Kennedy was the 3rd daughter, and was 16 when her father died.

On the 13th September 1895 she married a stockbroker named Francis Henry Ellissen whose father Adolf was of German decent. Francis was born 6th September 1868 and died on the 22nd April 1900 aged 31 in a special hospital.

They had two sons;

Myles Ashworth Ellissen born 19th August 1896 who went on to live in Canada, he was wounded in WWI and awarded the Military Cross. He died 10th September 1973 in Vancouver. He married firstly Helen Lethbridge Fraser (1896-1964) then in 1967 he married Beatrice Burroughs (b.16/6/1914-d.30/10/2011). He went on to buy a school and became its Headmaster.

Francis Kennedy Ellissen was born on 27th November 1898 in London and was a musician. He died in the USA on 15th October 1970.

In February 1913, aged 43, Elizabeth married the 24 year old Harry Bernard Wingate-White, an American from Los Angeles who adopted the boys but they kept their fathers name.

Francis Henry Ellissen

They lived in Canada where Harry died in 1961.

They are registered on a passenger liner visiting England in August 1915.

Elizabeth died on 28th July 1961 aged 94.

Myles Ellissen

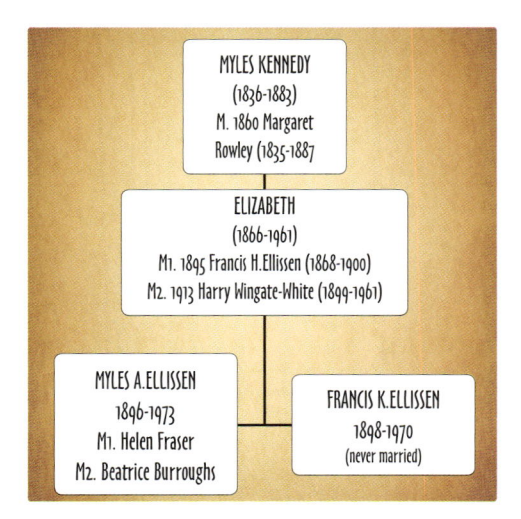

MYLES KENNEDY
(1836-1883)
M. 1860 Margaret Rowley (1835-1887)

ELIZABETH
(1866-1961)
M1. 1895 Francis H.Ellissen (1868-1900)
M2. 1913 Harry Wingate-White (1899-1961)

MYLES A.ELLISSEN
1896-1973
M1. Helen Fraser
M2. Beatrice Burroughs

FRANCIS K.ELLISSEN
1898-1970
(never married)

44

Chapter 10

FLORENCE CAMPBELL KENNEDY

Born 5th October 1867 • Died 24th February 1948 Aged 80
Married Name: Fisher

Florence Campbell Kennedy was the 4th daughter born on 5th October 1867 – She was 15 when her father died.

On the 12th February 1890 she married Charles Edward Fisher (born 1861 – died 19/12/1947) from Distington Hall. In the 1891 census Florence and Charles were living with his mother in Kensington.

They had three children;

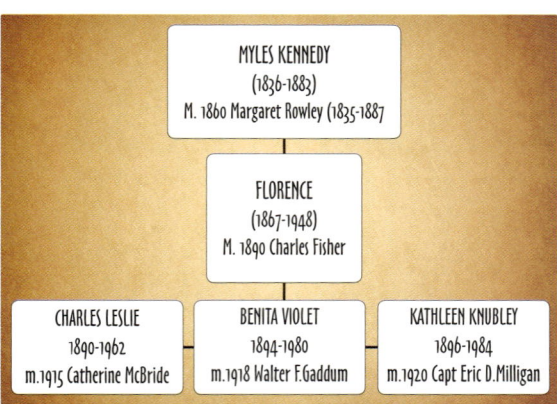

A son they named **Charles Leslie Fisher** who was born in December 1890. In the 1901 census he was at the same boarding school in Gosforth as Myles Storr Nigel Kennedy, his cousin. Then in 1915 he married Catherine, the only daughter of the Hon. Sir Peter McBride an Australian, with Scottish parents, who was on the board of mines in Australia. In 1913 he was in London as Agent General and was based here throughout the First World War. He and his wife, Mary (also his cousin), did a lot for Australian servicemen and their families during this time and lost one of their sons in action. He was knighted in 1915 & died suddenly

Charles (with Catherine seated) at Benita's wedding, Brockhole.

on March 3rd 1923 in Cannes which he visited as a keen sailor. He and his wife were decorated by the Serbian and Belgian governments for their wartime efforts. Charles Leslie Fisher later rose to the rank of Brigadier, he and Catherine had no children.

Their first daughter was **Benita Violet Fisher** born in 1894 who married Walter (Jim) Frederick Gaddum (1888-1956). Walter's family was a well-respected Manchester merchant family who settled in the Lake District after having Brockhole built on the shores of Lake Windermere. His mother was Edith Potter who was a double cousin of the famous Beatrix Potter. Beatrix often visited Brockhole and wrote letters to Walter and his sister Molly that have been published as part of her life.

Florence at Benita's coming out ball in 1912.

Walter (Jim) Gaddum & Benita on their wedding day in 1918 seen here at Brockhole with her sister Kathleen Fisher and cousin, Kathleen Trollope.

Kathleen Fisher was born in 1896 and married Captain Eric D Milligan. They had one son, David, born in 1931 but they later divorced. David went on to marry Daphne Hughes and they had four children. Kathleen, a gifted artist, died at her home in London in 1984.

Benita and Kathleen where noted as being bridesmaids at their cousin Sybil's wedding in 1916.

Florence died on 24th February 1948 aged 80.

With her son, David

Chapter 11

KATHLEEN KENNEDY

Born 3rd November 1868 • Died 31st July 1950 Aged 81
Married Name: Trollope

Kathleen Kennedy was born the 5th daughter on 3th November 1868 and was 14 when her father died.

She went on to marry Henry C Trollope (20/9/1859-13/7/1935), a surveyor and senior partner in George Trollope & Sons, on the 21st June 1893. She was given away by her brother Myles and her wedding reception was held by her sister Marguerite at her residence, Langley House.

She died much later than her husband on the 31st July 1950, outliving him by 15 years. They had 4 children;

Kathleen M Kennedy Trollope 1894-1979 m. Lt Col William Henry Fry (1885-1951)

Douglas Kennedy Trollope b.9th February 1897 in London and went onto the Royal Navy College where he became a Naval Cadet and later a Lieutenant. He died just after the end of WWI on 11th December 1918 whilst aboard HMS Tobago.

> **Trollope, Douglas Kennedy. R N Lieutenant Royal Navy H.M.S Tobago • Died Wednesday 11th December 1918, Aged 21 • Born 22 Cleveland Gardens, Paddington, London 9th February 1897 • 2nd son of Henry Charles Trollope and Kathleen Trollope (née Kennedy) of Haslemere, Littlestone-on-Sea, New Romney, Kent • Buried Dalmeny and South Queensferry Cemetery, Edinburgh, Scotland**

Douglas Kennedy Trollope memorial (grave ref 441)

Douglas Kennedy Trollope's commemoration on his parents' headstone at New Romney Cemetery, Kent. (2nd son should have read 2nd child).

Pamela Kennedy Trollope 1899 – 1990 m. Dr D.J.C. Ryder Richardson.

Marjorie Kennedy Trollope 1905 – 1939 m. Gerald Loup MC who retired as a Colonel.

Marjorie Kennedy Trollope

Pamela Kennedy Trollope

Chapter 12

MARY MAUDE KENNEDY

Born 24th November 1869 • Died 11th December 1936 Aged 67
Married Name: Trollope

The 6th daughter and was born on 24th November 1869, she was 13 when her father died.

She was 23 when she married John Evelyn Trollope in Sept 1893 who was an Architect and the brother of Charles Trollope who married her sister Kathleen. Within the Kennedy children, 2 brothers married 2 sisters from two different families. They had 3 children;

Myles Evelyn Trollope born 29th September 1894 who married Helen Norman on the 20th February 1924. He was made a 2nd Lt on 1st September 1914 and Captain on the 17th March 1920. They had two children, Patrick John Myles Trollope born 1925 and Shirley Frances Trollope born 1927 who both married.

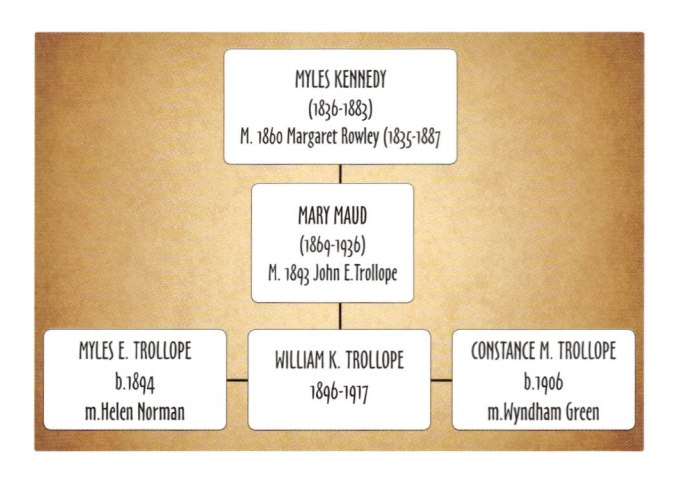

```
MYLES KENNEDY
(1836-1883)
M. 1860 Margaret Rowley (1835-1887)
            │
       MARY MAUD
       (1869-1936)
   M. 1893 John E. Trollope
            │
   ┌────────┼────────┐
MYLES E. TROLLOPE  WILLIAM K. TROLLOPE  CONSTANCE M. TROLLOPE
   b.1894              1896-1917              b.1906
m. Helen Norman                          m. Wyndham Green
```

William Kennedy Trollope

Born 8th May 1896 and was a 2nd Lieutenant in the Royal Navy Flying Corps. He was educated at Eastbourne and Uppingham and received his commission in the R.F.C in May 1916 being gazetted Flying Officer and proceeded to the front. Having been out over enemy lines, he was returning when he was attacked by five German planes at 5,000 feet. His observer was killed and he was wounded in the abdomen. He managed to land his plane just inside our lines but upside down. Still being shelled by the enemy a comrade went bravely out to bring Lt. Kennedy in. He found him alive but unconscious and in carrying him to safety, was himself dangerously wounded. William died 3rd May 1917 from wounds he received on the 3rd April 1917, he was just short of his 21st birthday and is buried the Aubigny Communal Cemetery, France.

Constance Margaret

Born 28th November 1906 and was married to Wyndam Green.

Mary Maude died on the 11th December 1936 aged 67.

Chapter 13

ALFRED ALEXANDER KENNEDY

Born 10th December 1870
Died 31st March 1926 Aged 55

Alfred Alexander Kennedy was 12 years old when his father died. He passed out as a Lieutenant and promoted to Captain in 1896. At the time Alfred was married he was a Captain in the 3rd Hussars and he served in the Boer War where he received the Queen's medal with 3 clasps.

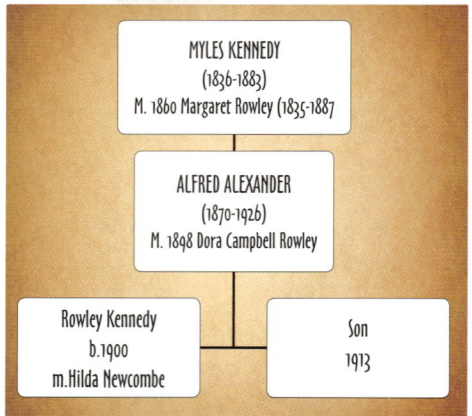

He progressed to become a Major in 1902, a Brigadier General in May 1915 and ended up a Major General. He was awarded a CMG in 1915 and a CB in 1921. During WWI he was mentioned in despatches 7 times and was involved with the first tank battles being fought in WWI under the direction of Sir Douglas Haig.

```
MYLES KENNEDY
(1836-1883)
M. 1860 Margaret Rowley (1835-1887)
        │
ALFRED ALEXANDER
(1870-1926)
M. 1898 Dora Campbell Rowley
        │
   ┌────┴────┐
Rowley Kennedy   Son
b.1900          1913
m.Hilda Newcombe
```

In Sir Douglas Haig's fifth dispatch he covered the Cambrai operations between Nov-Dec 1917 when the enemy captured Govzeaucourt at 9.00am and were advancing until they came up against the Guards, backed up by the 4th & 5th Cavalry divisions under the command of Major General Alfred Alexander Kennedy. They managed to push the enemy back and out of Govzeaucourt.

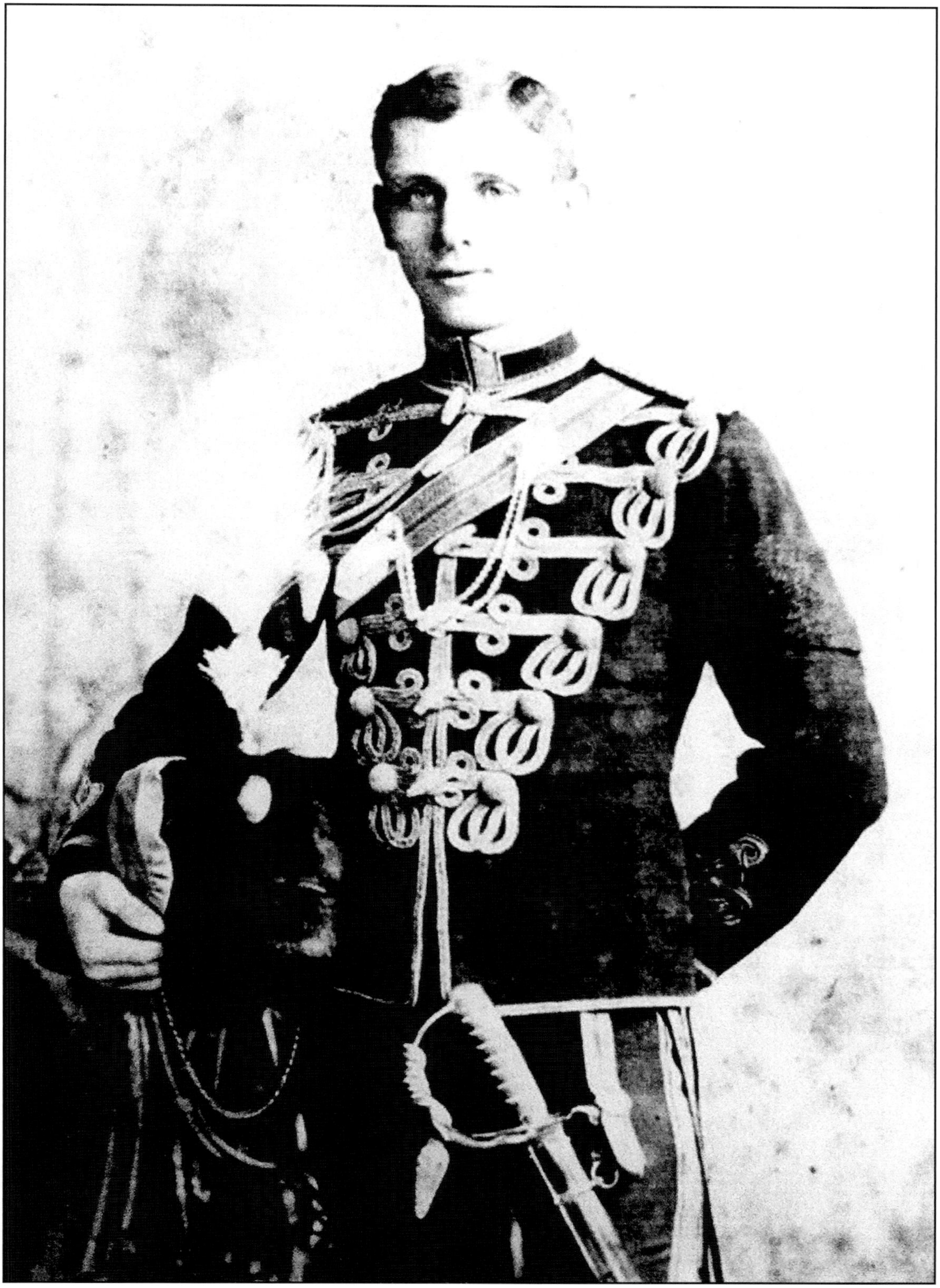

It was described by Sir Douglas as the greatest of gallantry acts and resolution as they made further progress to the East of the village. Earlier in 1915, whilst he was a Brigadier General he was noted in the battle order for the 2nd Ypes Battle Hill 60 as in command of the 7th Cavalry Brigade under Major General Hon JHG Byng and the Battle of Loos under Major General CJ Briggs. After a reorganisation of divisions he found himself involved in the ill fated battle of Ctesiphon (Iraq) between 22nd & 24th November 1915 whilst commanding the 6th Cavalry of the Anglo-Indian forces under General Sir John Nixon. In mid-summer 1918 he is mentioned in the battle plan for Aisne as commanding the 75th Brigade of the 25th Division.

Between 1919-1920 he held the post of Military Governor of Cologne and his was the name on posters that were displayed in December 1919 warning the Germans of Occupied Territory against sabotage of British telecommunications.

There are two portraits in the National Portrait Gallery of Alfred.

He also married his first cousin, Dora Campbell Rowley from Southport on the 5th July 1898. Dora was the youngest daughter of Walter T Rowley. Dora was born in 1874 and died 28th February 1952.

Proclamation | Bekanntmachung

1. Several cases have occurred of damage being done to British telephone and telegraph cable and appliances within the Occupied Territory.

2. If further such acts are committed and the responsible individuals are not at once discovered and apprehended, the British Military Authorities will inflict punishment on the community concerned.

3. It is therefore the duty of the civil population to give the British Military Authorities any information that may lead to the detection of the malefactors.

1. Es sind mehrere Fälle von Beschädigungen der britischen Telephon- u. Telegraphen-Leitungen u. -Apparate innerhalb des besetzten Gebietes vorgekommen.

2. Falls weitere solche Sachbeschädigungen begangen und die verantwortlichen Personen nicht sofort entdeckt werden, so wird der in Frage kommenden Gemeinde von der britischen Behörde eine Strafe auferlegt werden.

3. Es ist deshalb Pflicht der Zivil-Bevölkerung der britischen Militär-Behörde jede Mitteilung, welche zur Entdeckung der Täter führen kann, zu machen.

A. A. KENNEDY
MAJOR-GENERAL,
BRITISH MILITARY GOVERNOR
OCCUPIED GERMAN TERRITORY

They had two sons:

Rowley Kennedy

Born 30th March 1900 who went on to serve in the Royal Navy as a Lieutenant after studying at the Royal Navy College Osborne & Dartmouth. Rowley married a Hilda Newcombe on the 15th September 1923 and had a son named John Alistair Kennedy in 1931 and a daughter Penelope who was born 8th March 1928 but died on the 21st December 1938 aged 10.

Their second son was born and died in 1913.

Alfred died in York on the 31st March 1926 aged 55.

Hugh   Dolly Billinge   Alfred

Chapter 14

THEOBALD WALTER BUTLER KENNEDY

Born 12th December 1871
Died 12th August 1934 Aged 62

Theobald Walter Butler Kennedy was born the 4th son on the 12th December 1871, he was 11 years old when his father died.

He married his first cousin, Alice Campbell Rowley (Ethel's Sister) on 10th February 1903, interestingly the same date as his brother Myles and Ethel were married. Their wedding in Hawarden was a big affair with many guests including the Gladstone political family and his brother William George Ainslie Kennedy serving as Best Man, he was a Lt at the time.

Walter, as he was known, joined the navy at nearly 14 years old in 1885. In 1887 he was a Mid-Shipman aboard the Garnet. In 1897 he was aboard the Fearless, a twin screw cruiser, as a Lt. having been promoted to Sub-Lt previously. He then appeared as a Lt on the Kestral in 1901 which was a Torpedo boat destroyer. By 1902 he was aboard the Bulwork, a Battleship based in the Mediterranean Sea. In 1905 he served on the Albemarle before going onto the Barfleur as Commander. 1909 saw him on the Bacchante and 1913 the Royal Arthur. He was Captain of the Lowestoft, a light cruiser in 1914, which he stayed on for a few years. As Chief of Staff at the Nore under Admiral Sir Frederick C. Doveton Sturdee between 1918-1921 he held the rank of Flag Captain and Commodore.

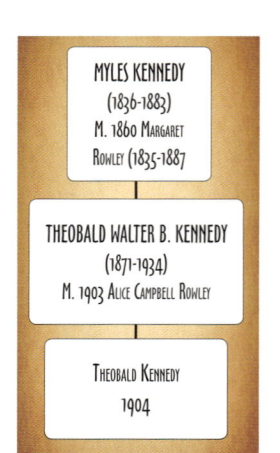

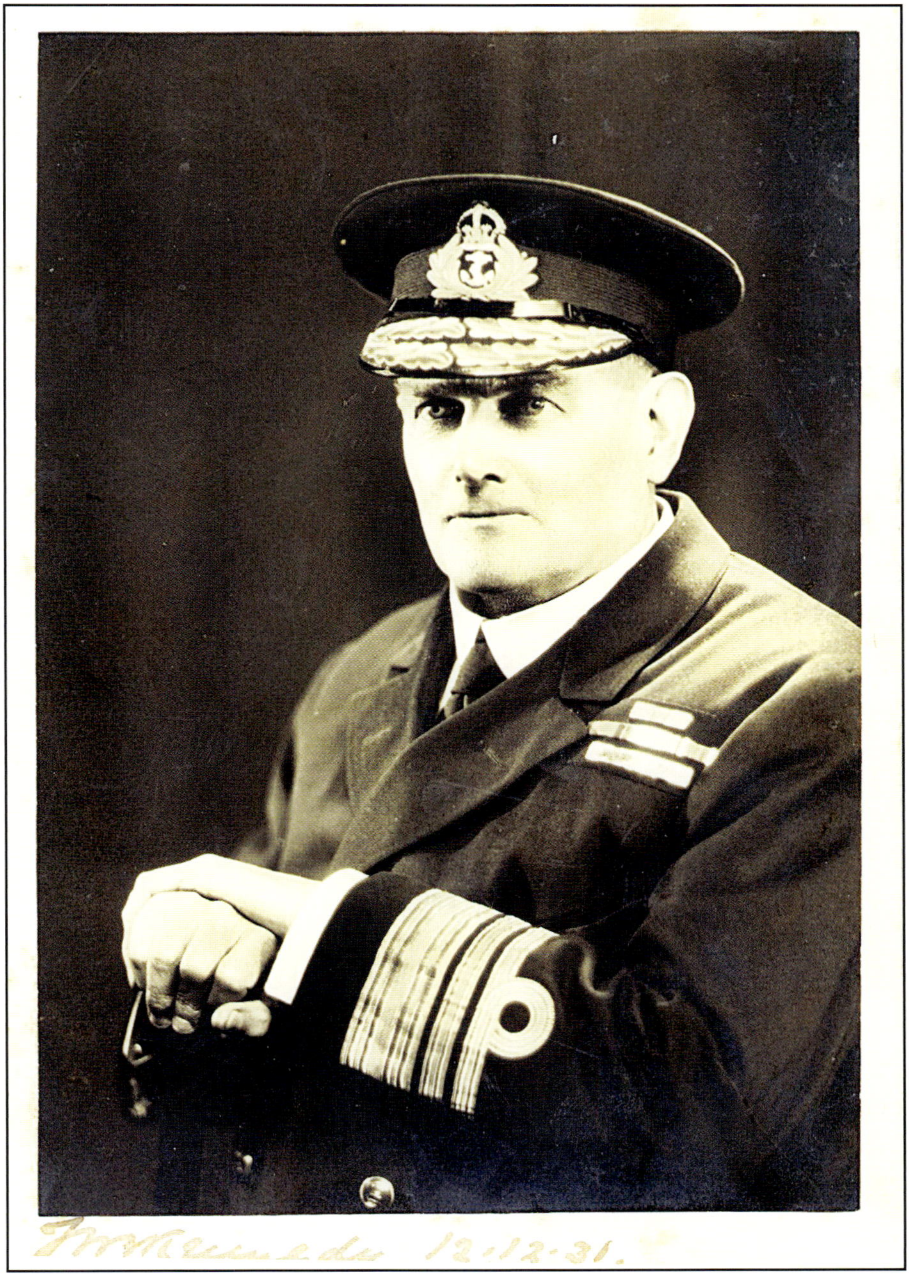
12.12.31.

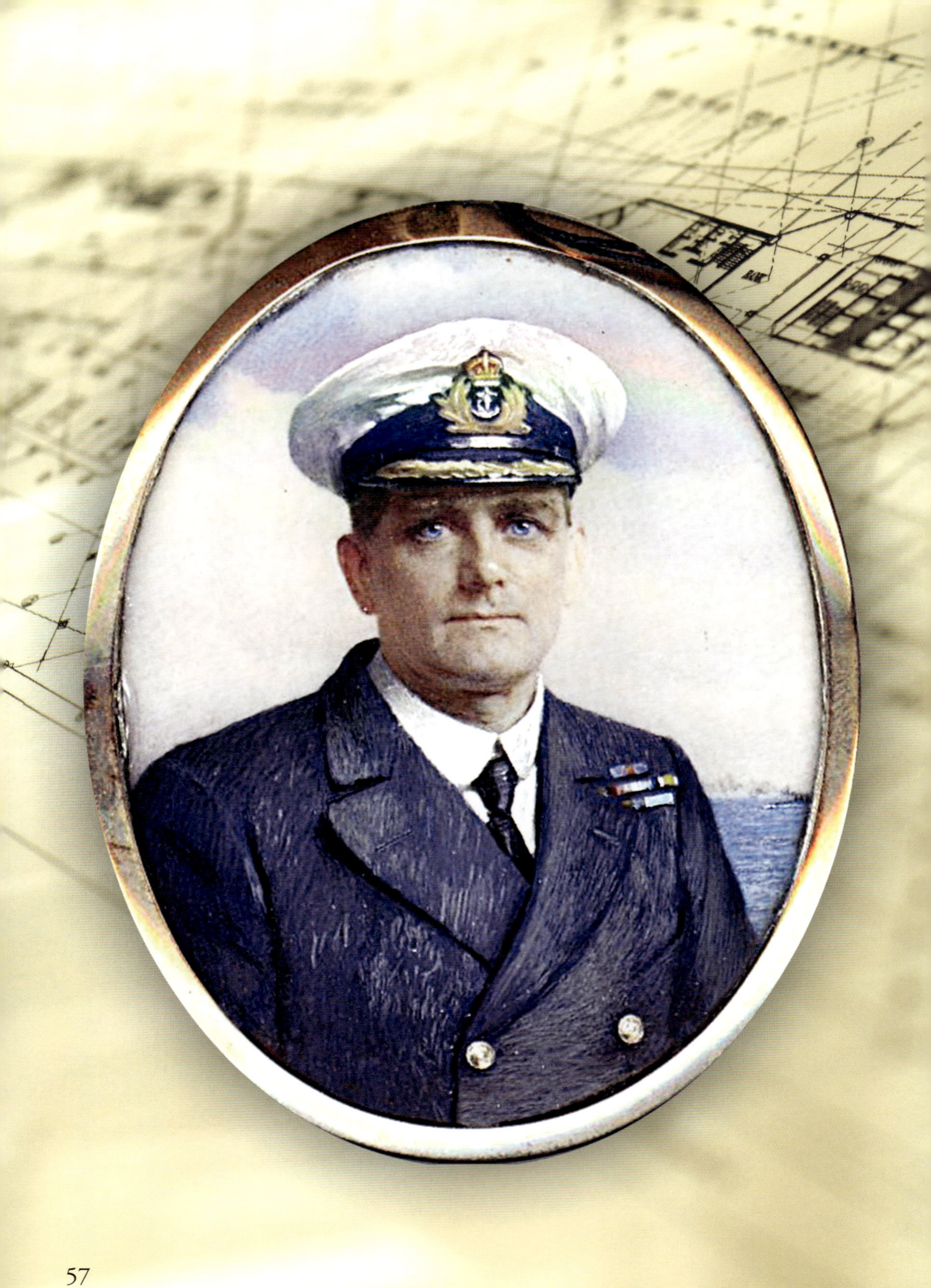

He became Rear Admiral on the 5th July 1921 and Vice Admiral on 25th October 1926.

Among his many awards he received the Order of Redeemer of Greece and was awarded a CMG on the 31st May 1918.

He and Alice had a son named Theobald who was born and died in August 1904.

Walter died on 12th August 1934 when he was 62 years old. His health must have been failing earlier as there is a letter held at Barrow-in-Furness records office written by him in January 1933 which was typed as he says he was not up to writing. In it, he was asking to arrange a loan against his shares in Kennedy Bros. as he states, *"I could not write a cheque for a single sovereign with the knowledge it would be met; my pension is ear-marked before I get it, a pleasant position for me to be in!"* and goes on to say how can't wait for the Kennedy Bros. dividend.

Walter (back row 2nd from left)
Alice - Sybil – Ethel (front row)

Chapter 15

VIOLET KENNEDY

Born December 1872 • Died 13th July 1956 Aged 84
Married Name: Maitland-Tower

Violet Kennedy was the 7th daughter, born in December 1872, she was 10 years old when her father died.

On the 7th June 1898 when she was around 26, she married Captain William Maitland Tower who was the only son of Major Francis Tower of Thremhall Priory Essex. William was born on the 9th July 1869 and died 13th June 1943. He was at Harrow in 1883 and later went on to serve with the 3rd Kings Own Hussars and left £43,000 in his will.

Later in life he was a JP and lived at Moreton House Oncar, they went on to have two children.

Firstly, **Alfred Francis Tower** was born in 1901 at the Curragh Camp in Ireland where his father was a Captain in the 3rd Hussars. By 1911 they were living at Cotefield Leighton Buzzard. He went to Malvern College passing out from Sandhurst, the Royal Military College, in December 1920 as a 2nd Lieutenant. In March 1921 he was wounded during the Crossbarry Ambush. One of the largest battles of the Irish War of Independence, 20km south west of Cork city, over 1000 British men were attempting to capture around 100 IRA men in a surprise attack. Tom Barry, the leading IRA officer, observed that one of the British Columns, under the command of the inexperienced Lt Tower, was ahead of the others and

Alfred Francis Tower

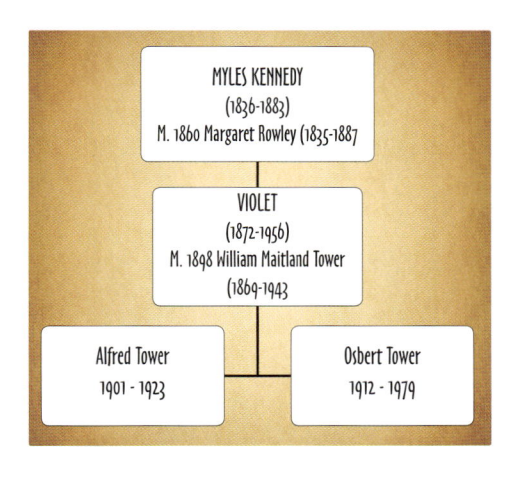

```
        MYLES KENNEDY
         (1836-1883)
M. 1860 Margaret Rowley (1835-1887)
              |
            VIOLET
          (1872-1956)
   M. 1898 William Maitland Tower
          (1869-1943)
          /         \
   Alfred Tower   Osbert Tower
    1901 - 1923    1912 - 1979
```

viewed this as a weak point in the British line and so laid out an ambush at the Crossbarry crossroads by planting mines. Although the mines were not wholly successful, the trucks that arrived were nearly empty of troops and when they were fired upon from close range the British took significant casualties and many fled. Setting fire to the trucks and gathering up the arms and ammunition left, the IRA men managed to escape having various fire fights along the way. On the British side 10 men died and several were wounded including Lt A.F.M. Tower. Alfred was seriously injured in the face and had to have several operations but made a great recovery and managed to return to his old unit with the Essex Regiment. He was stationed at Borden Camp when he suffered appendicitis and unfortunately died on the 9th June 1923. He was described by his senior officers as the best young officer in the regiment and was well respected by all ranks in everything he did.

The funeral took place at Fryerning and was with full military honours with his sword and cap placed on top of the Union Jack draped over the coffin. His Uncle, Major-General Alfred Alexander Kennedy and Aunties Emma Kennedy and Mable Hopwood (née Kennedy) attended.

He left his estate of £4,167 to his father, Major Tower.

Their other son, **Osbert Maitland Tower** was born in Feb 1912 and died in 1979.

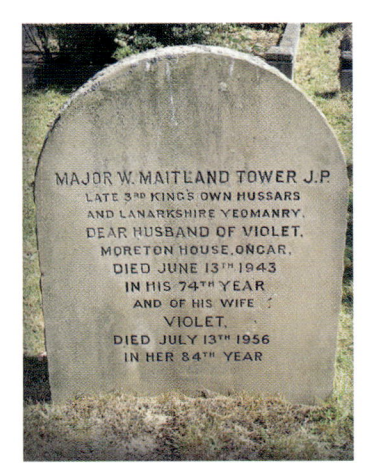

Violet died on 13th July 1956 at Red House, Waltham, Chelmsford aged 84. Her estate of £ 4,666 was left to her surviving son Osbert who at that time was a fruit farmer.

Chapter 16

WILLIAM GEORGE AINSLIE KENNEDY

Born 16th September 1873
Died 25th November 1938 Aged 65

William George Ainslie Kennedy was born the 5th son of Myles Kennedy on the 16th September 1873 and was 9 years old when his father died. He was named after his father's close friend, William George Ainslie, a partner in Harrison Ainslie & Co of Newlands.

He also joined the Royal Navy and by 15th November 1889 he was a Midshipman serving on HMS Australia after a brief spell aboard HMS Ruby the previous July. He was promoted to Sub-Lieutenant on the 14th October 1893 whilst studying at the Royal Naval College at Greenwich.

By July 1894 he was serving on HMS Thesus, before transferring to the twin-screw pre-dreadnought battleship HMS Centurion in 1896. This ship, which served as flagship of the China station, was under the command of Captain John Jellicoe, who went on to command the Grand Fleet at Jutland during the First World War.

Later that year he was promoted to Lieutenant and then, in 1898, transferred onto HMS Blake, a cruiser serving in the channel fleet.

He was aboard the cruiser HMS Niobe during the second Boer War (1899–1902), earning the Queen's and King's South Africa medal. He transferred to the light cruiser HMS Pioneer on the 18th April 1902 and then to the training ship HMS Nelson on the 11th March 1903. From there he went to serve aboard the Ardent-class twin-screw torpedo boat destroyer HMS Boxer, tendered to the depot ship HMS Vulcan in the Mediterranean, where, in 1907, he was promoted to Commander.

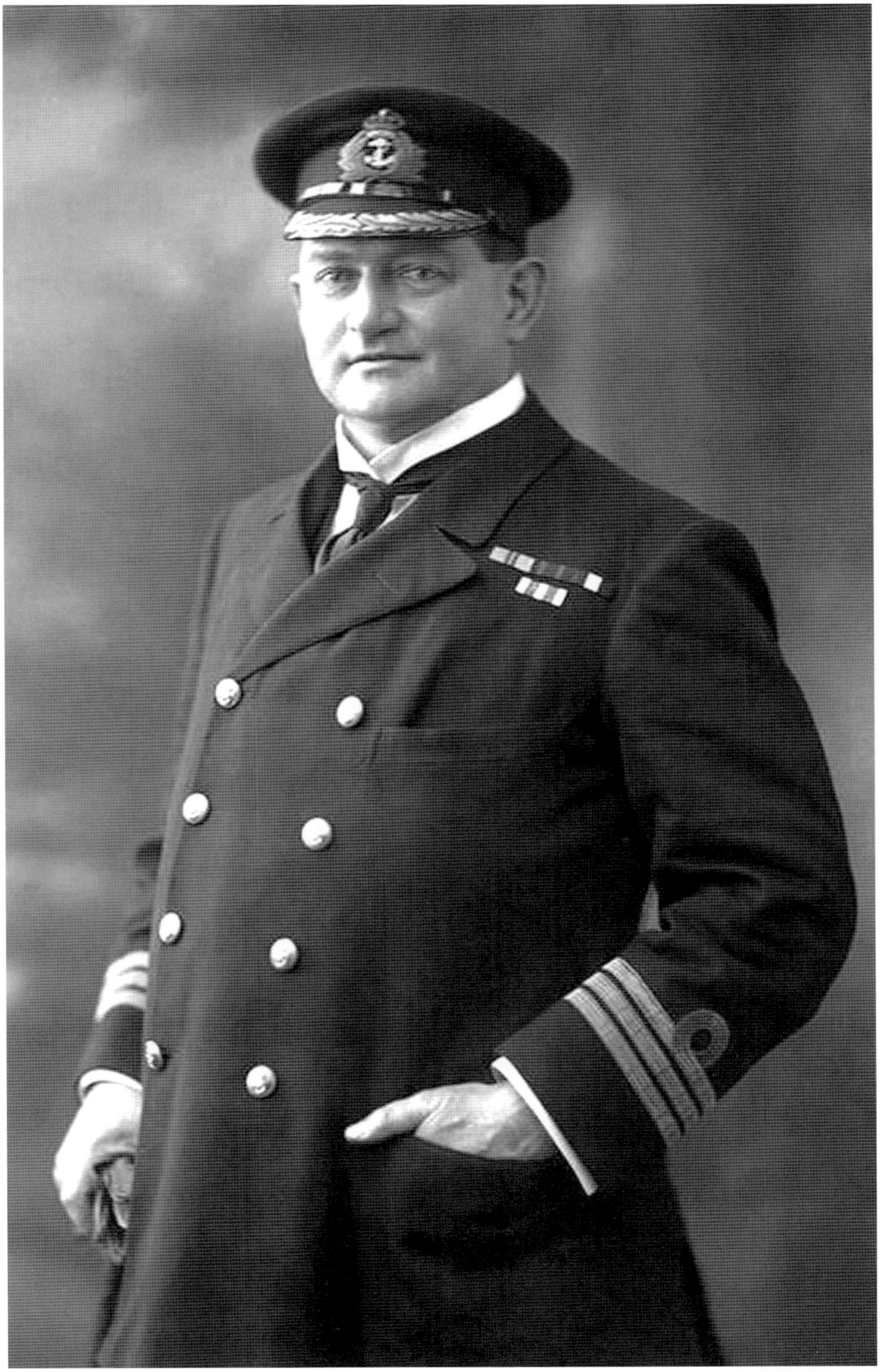

Subsequently he served aboard the Eclipse-class cruisers HMS Dido and HMS Minerva in 1908.

He was appointed as a Commander of the Order of the Crown of Italy (Commendatore dell'Ordine della Corona d'Italia) after assisting with the rescue of civilians following the Messina earthquake disaster in 1908 when serving on HMS Minerva. In 1911 he received the Coronation medal whilst in command of the Acorn-class destroyer HMS Minstrel. In 1914 he must have been seconded onto HMS India, a former P&O Cruiser converted into an armed merchant cruiser, when at the time he had been serving on the minelayer HMS Thetis. After the war he was in command of the cruiser HMS Diadem until 1920. He was promoted to Captain on the 22nd October 1921.

The most interesting episode of his Naval career took place during WWI when he was Commander of the armed merchant cruiser HMS India. On Sunday, 8th August 1915 the ship was sunk by the German U-Boat U22 in Norwegian waters with the loss of ten officers and 150 ratings. As Norway was a neutral country, he and the survivors were interned there for the rest of the war. William was responsible for his men and there were many cases of the survivors being allowed back to Britain on compassionate grounds, provided they did not take up military operations and returned within a month, but sometimes even this restriction was extended. It was here that he met and married on 28th February 1916 the younger Alice Fedora Lundh, who was the daughter of a Norwegian naval Commander who

The 'new' Mrs Kennedy

63

had himself served with the Royal Navy and married an Englishwoman. They had 2 sons, Myles Harold William Kennedy, who was born in April 1917, and Walter who died as a baby.

Myles, a keen sportsman, went on to be educated at RMC Sandhurst and fought in the battle of El Alamein where he suffered from wounds which resulted in the amputation of his right leg. He retired as a Major in the 4/7th Rajput Regiment of the Indian Army after marrying Martha Magdelena Conradie, a nurse who had cared for him after his injury during the war, on the 24th June 1944. They settled in South Africa and had 3 children.

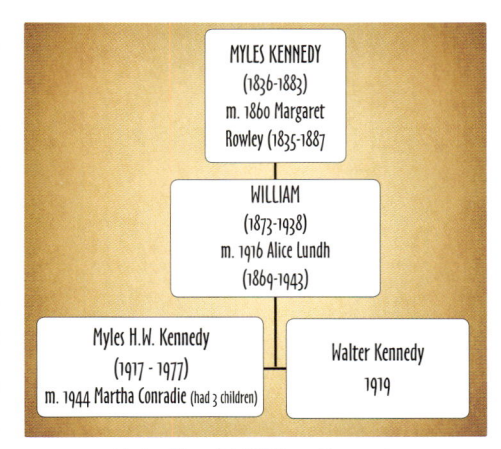

William kept a close association with Stone Cross and his brother Myles. He appears in several photos at Stone Cross in the early 1900's along with different cars he owned which seemed to be a great love of his. In the 1911 census he was staying at Stone Cross with Myles.

William died in Penrith on the 25th November 1938 aged 65 and left his estate of just over £3,000 to his wife, Alice. From the accounts of his life it seems William was viewed by all as a true gentleman.

MYLES KENNEDY (1836-1883)
m. 1860 Margaret Rowley (1835-1887)

WILLIAM (1873-1938)
m. 1916 Alice Lundh (1869-1943)

Myles H.W. Kennedy (1917 - 1977)
m. 1944 Martha Conradie (had 3 children)

Walter Kennedy 1919

Myles Harold William Kennedy

William George Ainslie Kennedy

Chapter 17

LUCY KENNEDY

Born 18th August 1874

Died 31st August 1874

Aged 13 days

Lucy Kennedy was born on the 18th August 1874, she was the 8th daughter, and died 13 days later on the 31st August. She is remembered in the family memorial at Holy Trinity Church Ulverston.

Chapter 18

EMMA LAW KENNEDY

Born 3rd September 1875
Died 1st February 1951 Aged 75

Emma Law Kennedy was born the 9th daughter on the 3rd September 1875, she was 7 years old when her father died.

Emma never married and appeared to spend a lot of time travelling, she is recorded as landing in Liverpool on the 13th June 1914 from Tenerife aboard S.S Benue.

She was known to be an excellent golfer playing off a very low handicap.

She attended the military funeral of her sister's son, Alfred Francis Towers and most of the family weddings.

She suffered with her health later in life and sadly spent the majority of her final years in a hospital where members of her family helped to support her financially.

She died 1st February 1951 aged 76 leaving her estate of £ 2,728 to her widowed sister Mabel Hopwood.

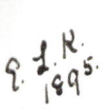

Chapter 19

MABEL KENNEDY

Born September 1876
Died 13th November 1954 Aged 78

Married Name: Hopwood

Mabel Margaret Kennedy was the youngest daughter of 10, born in September 1876, she was 6 years old when her father died.

After her father died it appears she and two of her sisters, Violet & Emma, went to live with their mother's sister, Jane Campbell Rowley in Flint. Aunty Jane must have helped bring them up as they were registered as living with her in the 1891 census and as she never married herself or had children, it appears she took to this role after their mother, Margaret, died in 1887. By 1901 Mabel was living on her own means in Braintree Essex.

On the 3rd July 1902 she married Geoffrey Hopwood (6/5/1877-14/8/1947). Geoffrey was a highly decorated son of Cannon Frank Edward Hopwood. Geoffrey became a Rear Admiral, was awarded a CBE and at one time was an ADC to George V along with being Deputy Director of Naval Intelligence.

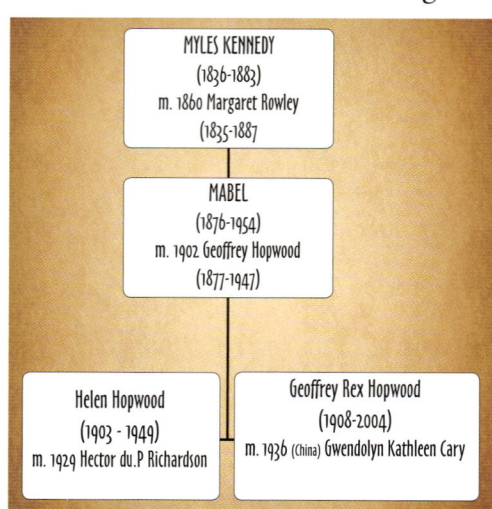

In the 1911 census she was living at 14 Royal Terrace Weymouth with their daughter Helen Joyce Hopwood born 15th February 1903 – died 4th July 1949. Helen married a Hector du. P Richardson (1901-1967) on 3rd August 1929, he was a Lt. Their son Geoffrey Rex Hopwood was born 1st April 1908 and died in 2004.

Mabel died 13th November 1954 aged 78.

```
MYLES KENNEDY
(1836-1883)
m. 1860 Margaret Rowley
(1835-1887)
        |
       MABEL
     (1876-1954)
m. 1902 Geoffrey Hopwood
     (1877-1947)
        |
   ┌────┴────┐
Helen Hopwood          Geoffrey Rex Hopwood
(1903 - 1949)              (1908-2004)
m. 1929 Hector du.P Richardson    m. 1936 (China) Gwendolyn Kathleen Cary
```

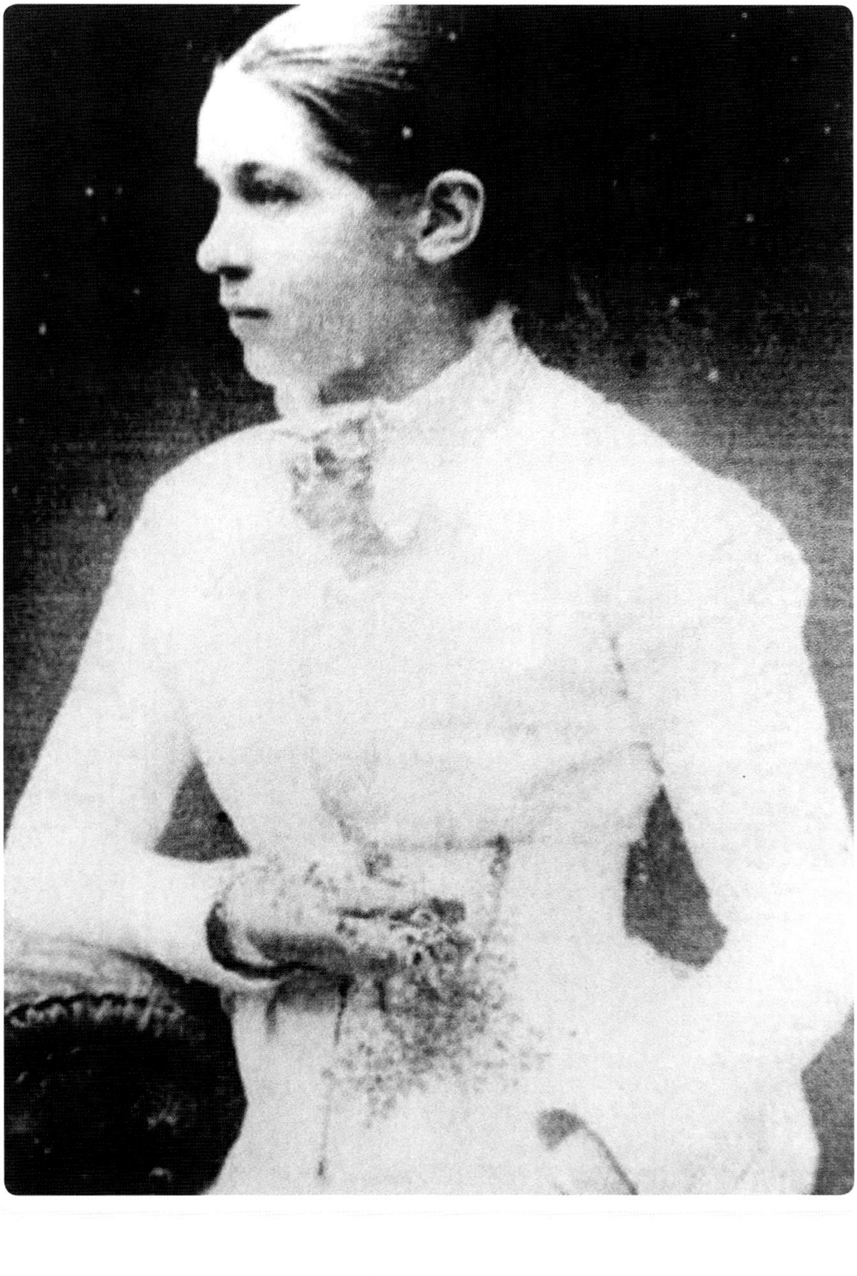

Chapter 20

ARTHUR HERBERT KENNEDY

Born 27th October 1877 • Died 26th August 1916 Aged 38

Arthur Herbert Kennedy was the youngest child born on the 27th October 1877 and he was 5 years old when his father died.

Along with his two sisters Elizabeth & Mary he was taken in by their elder sister Marguerite Rowley Kennedy who was living with her husband Henry C. Wilson in Langley House, Hastings, Sussex in 1891 with their 2 children. They went on to have another 6 children so pressure must have been on for her siblings to move on as soon as possible.

Arthur went on to be educated at Elstree School and later the Oxford Military College.

He married a nurse called Betty Alsopp, an Australian whose parents had already died before her marriage on February 10th (the same date as his brothers Myles & Theobald) 1900. It was an event for which the whole town turned out to see the happy couple as Arthur was due to go straight off to the Boer War, what a honeymoon! They were originally due to get married in Switzerland but when he got accepted to go to South Africa, it was the day before they were due to depart so decided to quickly arrange a wedding in Ulverston.

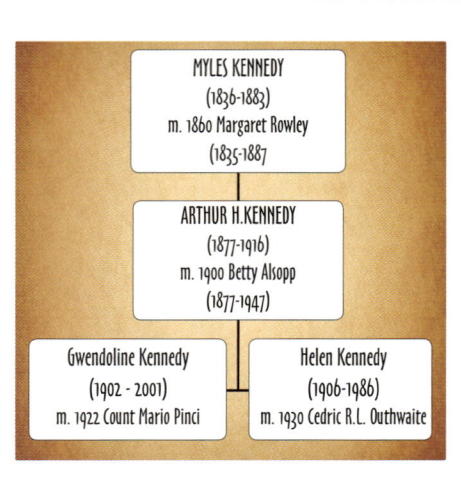

His new wife accompanied him to war and helped nurse the wounded.

He was a 2nd Lt in the 4th Battalion of the Kings Royal Lancaster Regiment in 1899.

He fought with General Buller's Army in the Boer War between 1899-1902 and received the Queens Medal with 5 Clasps.

Pte. Jones.   Pte. Penny.   Pte. Case.   Pte. Robinson.   Pte. Nicholson.

Photo by M. Groocock.
Pte. Gibson.   Corpl. Eckersley.   Lieut. Kennedy.   Pte. Garnett.   Lance-Corpl. Fletcher.

After a bit of travelling they settled in Australia around 1903 and set up as farmers in Colac, Victoria.

Like his brothers, Arthur was a keen sportsman being involved in cricket, horse racing, golf, sailing, shooting and rowing whilst Betty established the local the Red Cross.

Arthur Herbert Kennedy.

He was one of the original 7 officers who formed the Australian Imperial Force's 23rd Battalion as a Captain in 1915 and went to Egypt.

They served with the Mediterranean Expeditionary Force at Gallipoli and were involved with the evacuation of Lone Pine. They were then posted to France (26/3/1916) and he died from his wounds (probably pneumonia) as a POW on the 26/08/1916 in Hanover after a battle at

71

Taken on board HMAT Euripides en-route to Egypt May 30th 1915. Captain Kennedy (2nd row far left). Eight of these men were later killed in action

Pozieres Ridge on 28th July 1916. He was buried at Gottingen Cemetery (Neiderzwehren), his captors accorded him a full military funeral. Interestingly the battle was near Albert which is now twinned with Ulverston. He was 38 when he died.

His Commanding Officer wrote that due to the efficiency of his Company they were marked down for the most dangerous and important missions since the Regiment had been on active service. They were the party last to leave the evacuation of Lone Pine, right and most dangerous flank on the canal, left flank at Armentieres and lastly in the lead at Pozieres. No other casualty in the Regiment had caused more genuine regret than that of Captain Kennedy who was seen as a true leader of men.

Through this time Betty had followed him to Egypt, (Gwen was at school in England and Helen left with relatives in Australia) but when he was posted to France, Betty returned to Australia to collect Helen. On the journey from Australia to England in 1916 she learned at their first port of call that Arthur was missing believed killed, at their second port of call that he was alive and a POW and at their final port of call that he had died from his wounds. Bessie and the girls returned to Australia until 1922 when they headed back to England. Bessie then settled in the South of France and there are letters in the records office where she is disputing tax bills from her dividends in Kennedy Bros. In 1939 she moved back to England to rent stables and was joined by Helen. They had a large extended family with their cousins at this stage with the Frys, Milligans and Loups often all getting together. Horses seemed to be a lifelong passion for the girls dating back to their early Australian upbringing.

War Memorial in Osmotherley, Cumbria with a mention to A.H. Kennedy

He was mentioned in despatches, twice. Secondly in the London Gazette by Sir Douglas Haig on the 04/01/1917. He was recommended for the DSO in 1915.

He is remembered in Panel 99 in the Australian War Memorial.

In his will he left an estate of £ 15,435.

They had 2 daughters,

Gwendoline Kennedy

b. 21/10/1902 and became a Countess after she married Italian, Count Mario F.C. Pinci, MAV, DSO, MBV, MC, C de G, C diG, of Rome (born 2/9/1896-died 2/4/1987) on the 18th July 1922 in London. They met on the boat from Australia when Bessie was removing Gwen from a relationship with a young man that she deeply disapproved. Mario was the eldest son of Comandatore Giovanni Pinci. They lived on the outskirts of Paris throughout the Second World War where they were under the watchful eye of the Gestapo due to Gwen's background. After the capitulation of Italy they felt the need to escape and walked across the Pyrenées to Spain but returned to France after the war.

Their son **Michele Arthur Kennedy Pinci** was born in 1923 in England and went to Sherborne School. During WWII he was assigned to the 2nd SAS and during Operation Wallace, when helping the French Resistance, he was fired upon by his own Allied aircraft whilst travelling in an unmarked car. He died of his wounds on 11th September 1944 and is buried in Hauts-de-Seine Cemetery. They also had a daughter called **Rossana** (born 1930) who spent the war years in England with her Grandmother and went on to marry an Italian named Gingin Vigano, they had a daughter who lives in Florence.

Michele 'Micky' Pinci

Helen Wentworth Kennedy

b.10/09/1906 went to finishing school in Switzerland and married Cdr Cedric Robert Leonard Outhwaite DSC RNVR on the 5th May 1930. He died 2/10/1945 and was the son of Robert Leonard Outhwaite, an Australian MP from Melbourne. They had a son named **Brian Robert Outhwaite** on the 29th September 1931 who was also educated at Sherborne and became a Lt Cdr in the Royal Navy. He married Diane Beaumont, only daughter of Col.Hon. Ralph Edward Blackett Beaumont CBE of Montgomeryshire. They went on to have their own children.

Chapter 21

HOLY TRINITY CHURCH ULVERSTON

Holy Trinity Church has long been associated with the Kennedys, starting with the first baptism performed there of Harriet Kennedy, daughter of Charles Storr and Elizabeth Kennedy on 28th March 1832.

They were great beneficiaries and had several memorial windows installed over time.

One window which was originally installed in the East end of the church in 1870 had three lights. It was re-installed in 1880 after alteration work to the Chancel. It was donated by Mrs Kennedy of Fair View in conjunction with her son Myles then of Hill Foot and later Stone Cross in memory of Charles Storr Kennedy who died in 1857 and their son Charles Burton Kennedy of Kirklands who died in 1865, both of who were interred in the churchyard. The window itself bore no identification of the donor or object when it was first erected but a brass plate underneath read, 'Dedicated to the memory of a Husband and a Son and of a Father and a Brother.' The window itself was represented by several religious scenes.

The window at the East end of the South aisle was presented to the church in November 1881 by Myles Kennedy then at Stone Cross in memory of his Mother, Elizabeth who died in 1872. It consisted of two compartments. The lower one depicting the entrance of the Virgin Mary into the house of Zacharias. The upper one showing the visit of the Three Holy Women on the morning of the resurrection with the dedicated legend,

'In memory of Elizabeth, widow of Charles Storr Kennedy Esq. JP.'

The third window, which was installed in the South wall adjacent to the one just mentioned was also presented by Myles in memory of the Rev. G Pickering, the second incumbent of Holy Trinity for 34 years who died in 1873. It had two compartments, one of John the Baptist in the wilderness the other of the Apostle Paul preaching at Athens.

In October 1883 the Freemasons of Furness erected a memorial window in the memory of Myles Kennedy of Stone Cross who had died in that March. It had two compartments, the upper one showing the Wisdom of King Solomon, the lower showing the building of the temple at Jerusalem with the 'All seeing Eye' above and showing Masonic symbols within it.

The Latter windows were executed by Messrs Powell Bros of Leeds, the same firm were commissioned by Mrs Kennedy of Stone Cross to fill the West window with stained glass in memory of her late husband and was erected in August 1884.

A monthly magazine was produced by the church called the *Trinitarian*.

Chapter 22

STONE CROSS MANSION
ULVERSTON

Stone Cross Mansion was the vision of Myles Kennedy who was living at Hill Foot at the time, having decided not to purchase Conishead Priory. It was reported that he had spent £41,000 by the time he was at the first floor level. Designed by James Wright Grundy, with some possible influence off Paley & Austin and built by James Garden, it was based on a Gothic/Scottish Baronial style and built of limestone with Hexham freestone quoins. He also designed Croftlands and Lynne Dene in Ulverston but Stone Cross was seen as his chief work.

Stone Cross (South front view) in 1910

Myles would have probably starting planning Stone Cross in the early 1870's when his family was large, although there were more children to come. The reception rooms and principal bedrooms were designed around the central arcade with the north-west corner being the service wing area with separate narrow staircases installed so staff could move around the house from the cellar to the attic spaces without being seen. In more modern times musical recitals have been performed in the stair hall and as Myles was a lover of the arts, he may have had this in mind for his original design brief.

Sleeping Beauty

Started in 1874 and completed around 1879 it was furnished with lavish furniture and paintings and included a re-production of Tennyson's Sleeping Beauty signed by Lucien Besche in 1880 with family members and friends believed to be depicted in the faces.

As you enter through the front porch you first encounter an Anti-room on your right for guests to wait in whilst their coats where taken to a cloakroom on the left on the entrance. You then enter into the main hall where a sweeping oak staircase would take you up to the first floor level around the arcade. The hall is paved with Minton's Tiles of a special design that were laid by their own workmen. Looking up you would have seen the Lantern Light filled with ornamental stained glass. Around the hall are fine polished marble columns with intricate carvings of nature scenes which support the moulded arches made of fine Hare Hill Stone.

There are four principal rooms off the Hall, The Dining Room (39ft x 22ft) covered mainly in Dantzic Oak and having a large fire place also housed the same type of marble columns which separated a bay which the servants laid out for a sideboard arrangement from which they could access the kitchens.

Across the corridor was the Drawing Room (26ft x 22ft) with its ornate ceiling having the mouldings of the Kennedy Crest in the central section. This room would have enjoyed views of the rose gardens, before an extension was added, a lot later. You could then enter the Saloon (48ft x 18ft), which was originally only accessed from the main hall but later was connected at both ends to the Drawing room and Morning room.

The Saloon looked out onto the ornate glass conservatory and the eastern views of the lawn areas.

Saloon without furniture

Saloon with furniture

The Morning room (26ft x 22ft), or as it was to be known later, 'The Boudoir'. Again with the same ornate ceilings, was a principal room.

The Morning Room or 'Boudoir'

If you turned left from the main entrance you pass several large family rooms with a separate entrance. These rooms were likely to have been the Library, Smoking room and Study rooms where Myles could have entertained his business and social associates.

Study room

Library

At the end of the corridor is a large well lit Billiard room that must have been a focal point for entertaining.

The Billiard Room

On the opposite side of this corridor there are several small offices which would have been occupied by those running the house. These office rooms had views out to the external yard and easy access to the front of house and main areas with a separate stairs to the cellar and upstairs areas.

The separate entrance leading to the family rooms

The Kitchen

Further along you pass the various store rooms and staff dining room on your way to what would have been a very modern kitchen.

There is also another service stairs which is very narrow and obviously used by servants to move about the house and their quarters.

There were three staircases that gave access to the cellar areas that are vast and would have housed Myles' extensive wine collection along with other meat stores and pantries. There is a separate entrance to the basement in the service yard. The cellar also housed a 32ft x 29ft children's recreation room with its own staircase entrance.

As you glide up the wide oak stairs you can turn left or right on the first landing that would take you onto an Arcade area, you would have been faced with three oil paintings in 11ft x 6ft recesses that re-tell Tennyson's Sleeping Beauty, executed by Lucien Victor Besche.

Sleeping Beauty

84

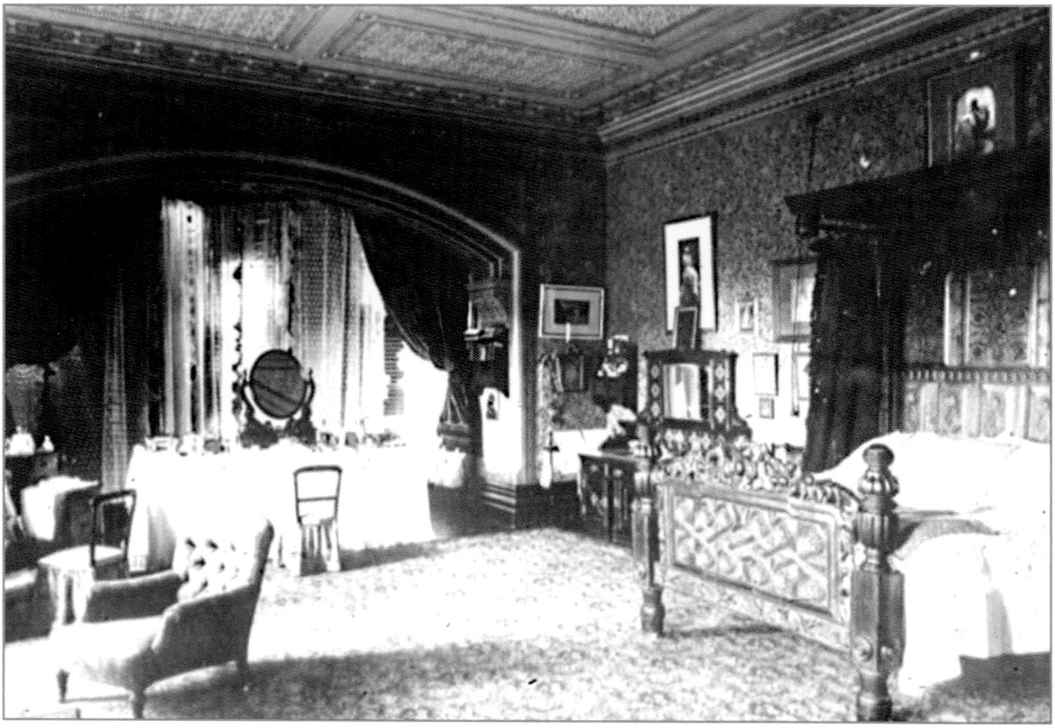

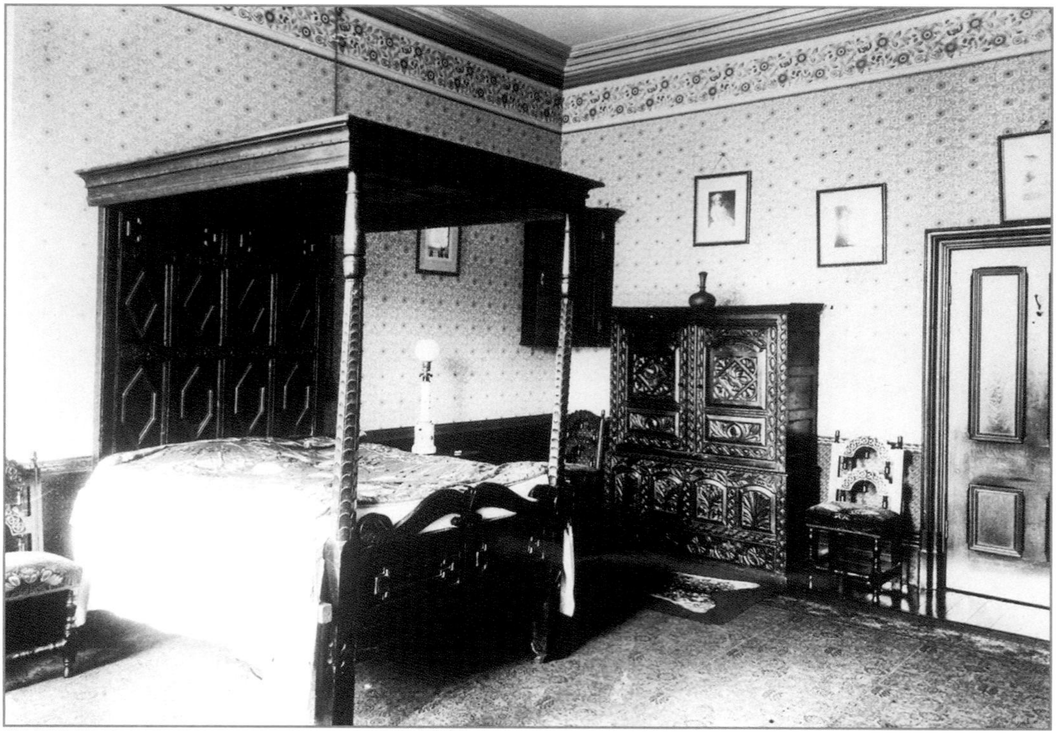

The first floor housed 14 bedrooms, 4 of which had had dressing rooms and bathrooms en-suite and three others with attached dressing rooms.

The second floor housed 16 bedrooms with various box and luggage rooms along with linen and housemaid closets and boasted hot and cold water. At one point there was a hydraulic lift that connected each floor.

From the master bedroom there is a private staircase that leads up the observation tower at the top. At the time of being built this would have enjoyed extensive views in all directions.

The stables housed 7 stalls and 3 loose boxes with harness and cleaning rooms attached. Along with two sleeping rooms, straw, hay and corn lofts and running hot water, they were first class.

The grounds also housed several lodges and had a large coach house with revolving shutters and a spacious enclosed yard with a glass covered shed for carriage washing.

When Myles died in 1883 he left his estate to be managed by his wife. To me this showed that their marriage seemed to be a partnership rather than a marriage of convenience or similar arrangements that were in place in those times. Upon Margaret's death in 1887 Stone Cross and its belongings were put up for auction. This seemed strange to me but may have been a normal procedure for the time. I would have thought that the house and its belongings would have just passed to Mylie (Myles) as the eldest son. As stated previously, he was the main beneficiary but he must have had to sell possessions to provide the split of the estate as per his father's wishes. A lot of fixtures and fittings were retained as shown in photographs from the early 1900's which indicates that Mylie must have bought a lot of them back.

The mansion was originally put up for sale in 1888 but no buyer was found so they tried again in 1896, this suggests that as no private buyer could be found after Margaret's death in 1887 the house could have been empty for the 8 years in between. As Mylie was in occupation in the late 1890's I assume he must have bought it. His brothers were often in attendance over the next 20 years so maybe a deal was done which settled how the estate was to be distributed.

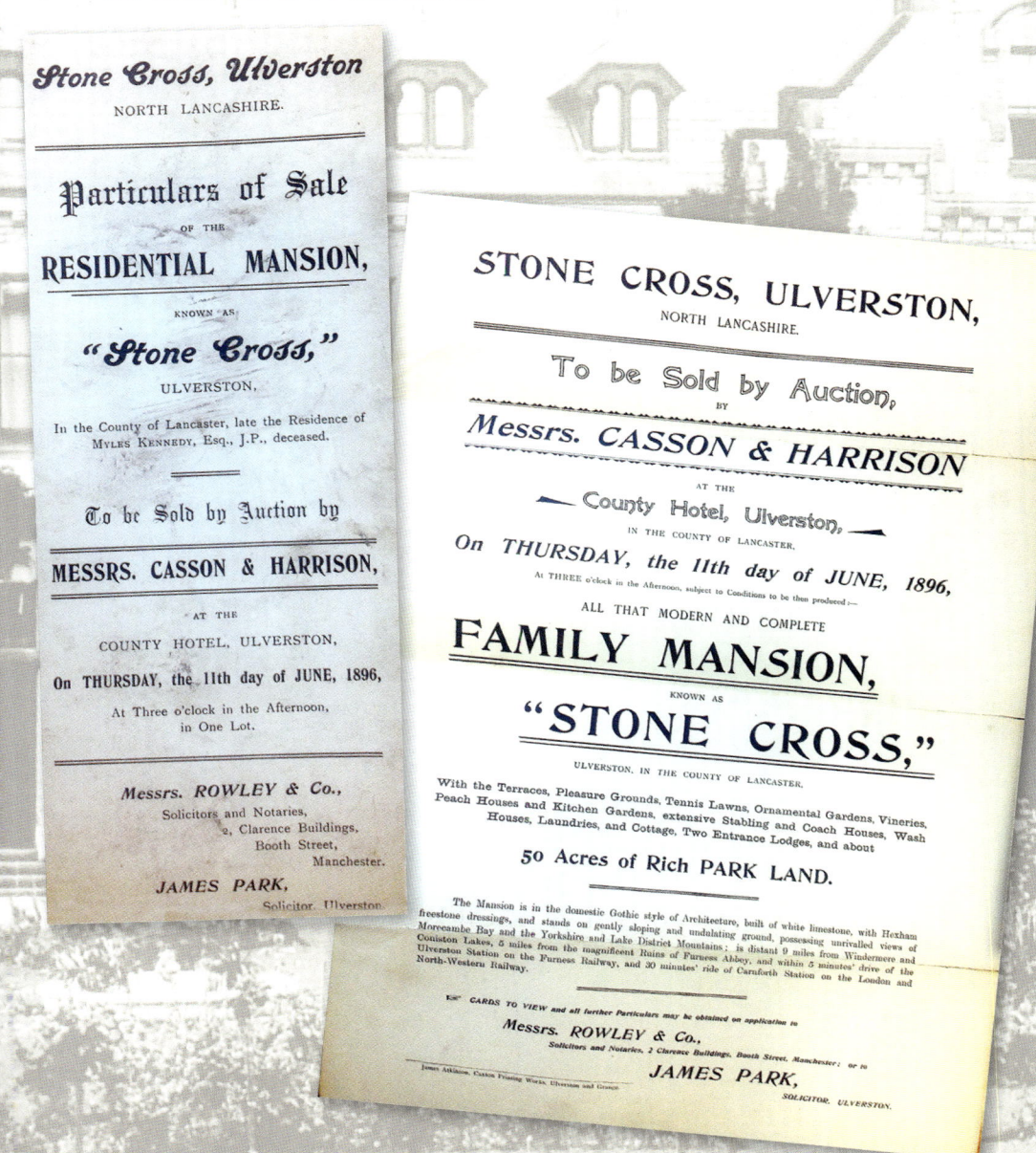

Stone Cross, Ulverston
NORTH LANCASHIRE.

Particulars of Sale
OF THE
RESIDENTIAL MANSION,
KNOWN AS
"Stone Cross,"
ULVERSTON,
In the County of Lancaster, late the Residence of
MYLES KENNEDY, Esq., J.P., deceased.

To be Sold by Auction by
MESSRS. CASSON & HARRISON,
AT THE
COUNTY HOTEL, ULVERSTON,
On THURSDAY, the 11th day of JUNE, 1896,
At Three o'clock in the Afternoon,
in One Lot.

Messrs. ROWLEY & Co.,
Solicitors and Notaries,
2, Clarence Buildings,
Booth Street,
Manchester.
JAMES PARK,
Solicitor, Ulverston.

STONE CROSS, ULVERSTON,
NORTH LANCASHIRE.

To be Sold by Auction,
BY
Messrs. CASSON & HARRISON
AT THE
County Hotel, Ulverston,
IN THE COUNTY OF LANCASTER,
On THURSDAY, the 11th day of JUNE, 1896,
At THREE o'clock in the Afternoon, subject to Conditions to be then produced:—
ALL THAT MODERN AND COMPLETE
FAMILY MANSION,
KNOWN AS
"STONE CROSS,"
ULVERSTON, IN THE COUNTY OF LANCASTER.

With the Terraces, Pleasure Grounds, Tennis Lawns, Ornamental Gardens, Vineries, Peach Houses and Kitchen Gardens, extensive Stabling and Coach Houses, Wash Houses, Laundries, and Cottage, Two Entrance Lodges, and about

50 Acres of Rich PARK LAND.

The Mansion is in the domestic Gothic style of Architecture, built of white limestone, with Hexham freestone dressings, and stands on gently sloping and undulating ground, possessing unrivalled views of Morecambe Bay and the Yorkshire and Lake District Mountains; is distant 9 miles from Windermere and Coniston Lakes, 5 miles from the magnificent Ruins of Furness Abbey, and within 5 minutes' drive of the Ulverston Station on the Furness Railway, and 30 minutes' ride of Carnforth Station on the London and North-Western Railway.

☞ CARDS TO VIEW and all further Particulars may be obtained on application to
Messrs. ROWLEY & Co.,
Solicitors and Notaries, 2 Clarence Buildings, Booth Street, Manchester; or to
JAMES PARK,
SOLICITOR, ULVERSTON.

James Atkinson, Caxton Printing Works, Ulverston and Grange.

On Friday the 24th & Saturday 25th June 1910 they held a Country Fair in aid of Consumption at Stone Cross, some of the lavish brochures still exist today.

89

Mylie stayed in occupation until his death in 1928 and Ethel continued there until her death in 1943. Their sons continued to live at Fair View and Hill Foot and Stone Cross was used by the military during WWII eventually being sold to Lancashire County Council in 1946.

STONE CROSS MANSION AFTER THE KENNEDYS

Lancashire County Council set about converting it and added some unsympathetic extensions and alterations including the removal of the lower flight of the grand staircase to enable them to play football in the main hall.

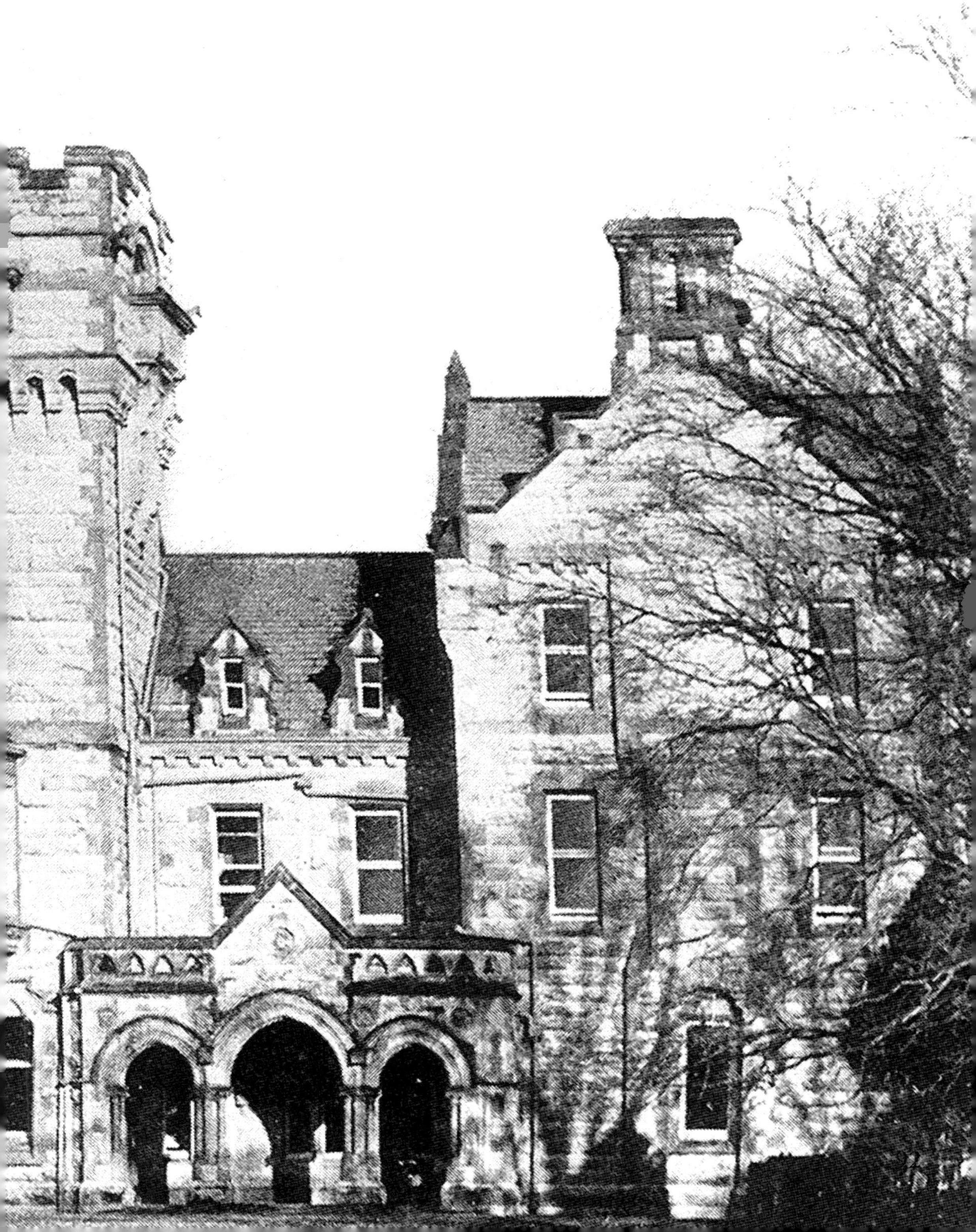

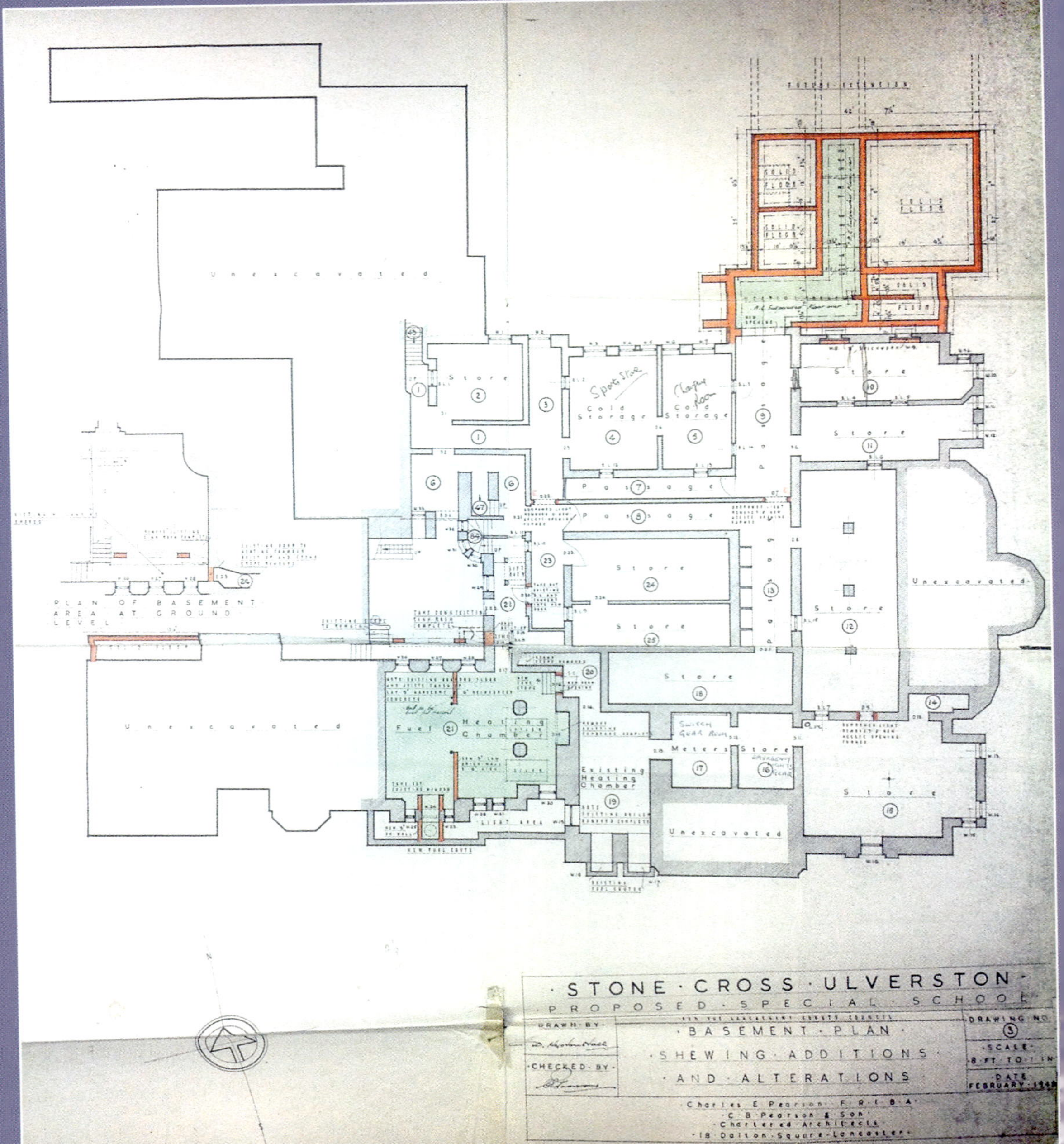

Unexcavated
Store
Cold Storage
Cold Storage
Passage
Passage
Store
Store
Store
Store
Store
Store
Store
Unexcavated
PLAN OF BASEMENT AREA AT GROUND LEVEL
Unexcavated
Fuel
Heating Chamber
Existing Heating Chamber
Meters
Store
Store
Unexcavated
· STONE · CROSS · ULVERSTON ·
· PROPOSED · SPECIAL · SCHOOL ·
DRAWN · BY ·
CHECKED · BY ·
· BASEMENT · PLAN ·
· SHEWING · ADDITIONS ·
· AND · ALTERATIONS ·
DRAWING NO
3
· SCALE ·
8 FT TO 1 IN
· DATE ·
Charles E Pearson · F · R · I · B · A ·
· C · B · Pearson & Son ·
· Chartered Architects ·
· 18 · Dalton · Square · Lancaster ·

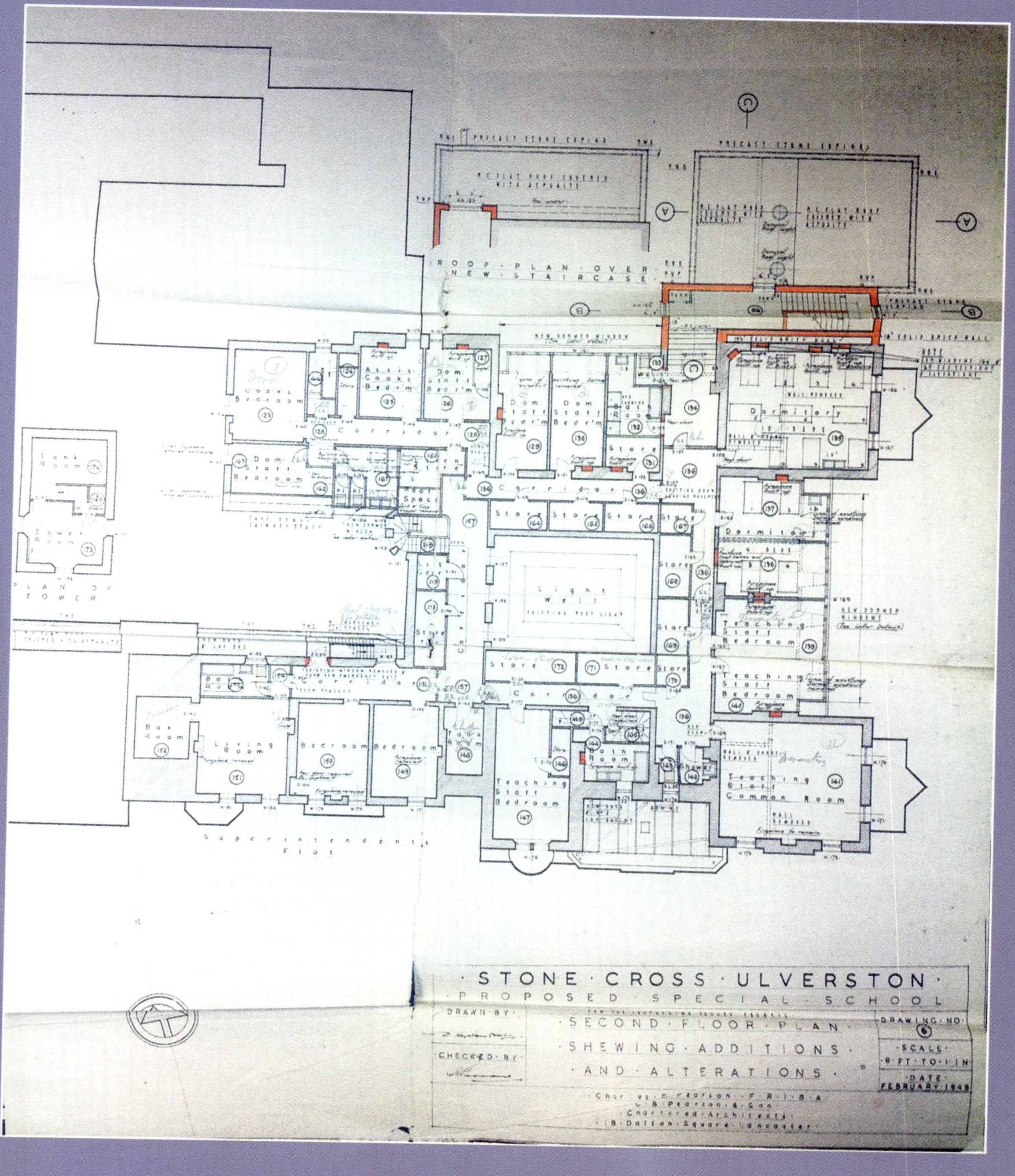
ROOF · PLAN · OVER · NEW · STAIRCASE
Light Well
Superintendent's Flat
PLAN OF TOWER
· STONE · CROSS · ULVERSTON ·
· PROPOSED · SPECIAL · SCHOOL
DRAWN · BY ·
CHECKED · BY ·
· SECOND · FLOOR · PLAN ·
· SHEWING · ADDITIONS ·
· AND · ALTERATIONS ·
DRAWING · NO ·
6
· SCALE ·
8 · FT · TO · 1 · IN
· DATE ·
FEBRUARY 1948
C B Pearson & Son
Chartered Architects
18 Dalton Square Lancaster

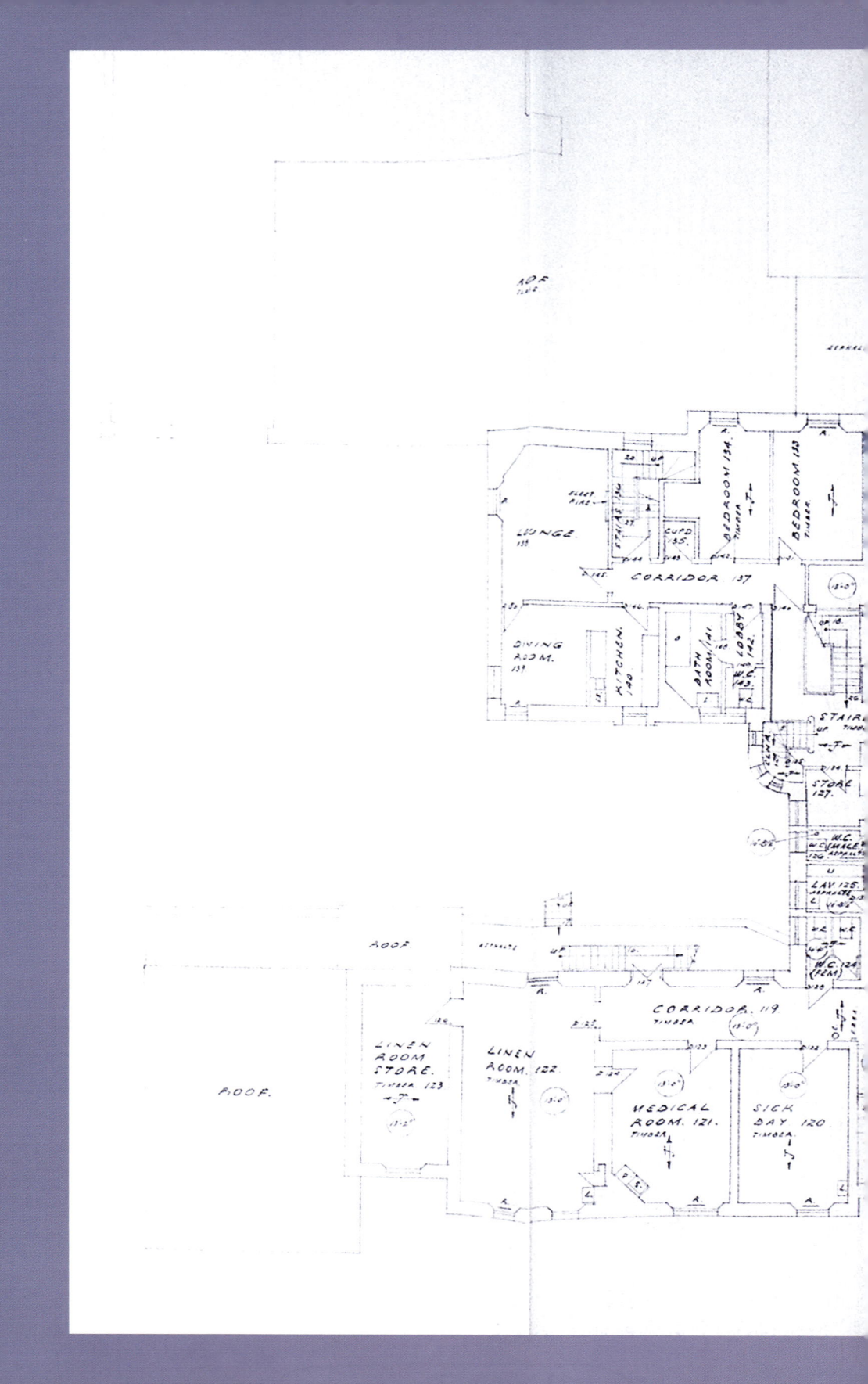
ROOF.
LOUNGE.
CORRIDOR 137
BEDROOM 134
BEDROOM 133
CUPD 135.
DINING ROOM. 139
KITCHEN. 140.
BATH ROOM. 141
LOBBY 142.
W.C. 143
STORE 127.
LAV 125.
ROOF.
CORRIDOR. 119.
TIMBER
LINEN ROOM STORE.
TIMBER 123
LINEN ROOM. 122.
TIMBER.
ROOF.
MEDICAL ROOM. 121.
TIMBER.
SICK DAY 120
TIMBER.

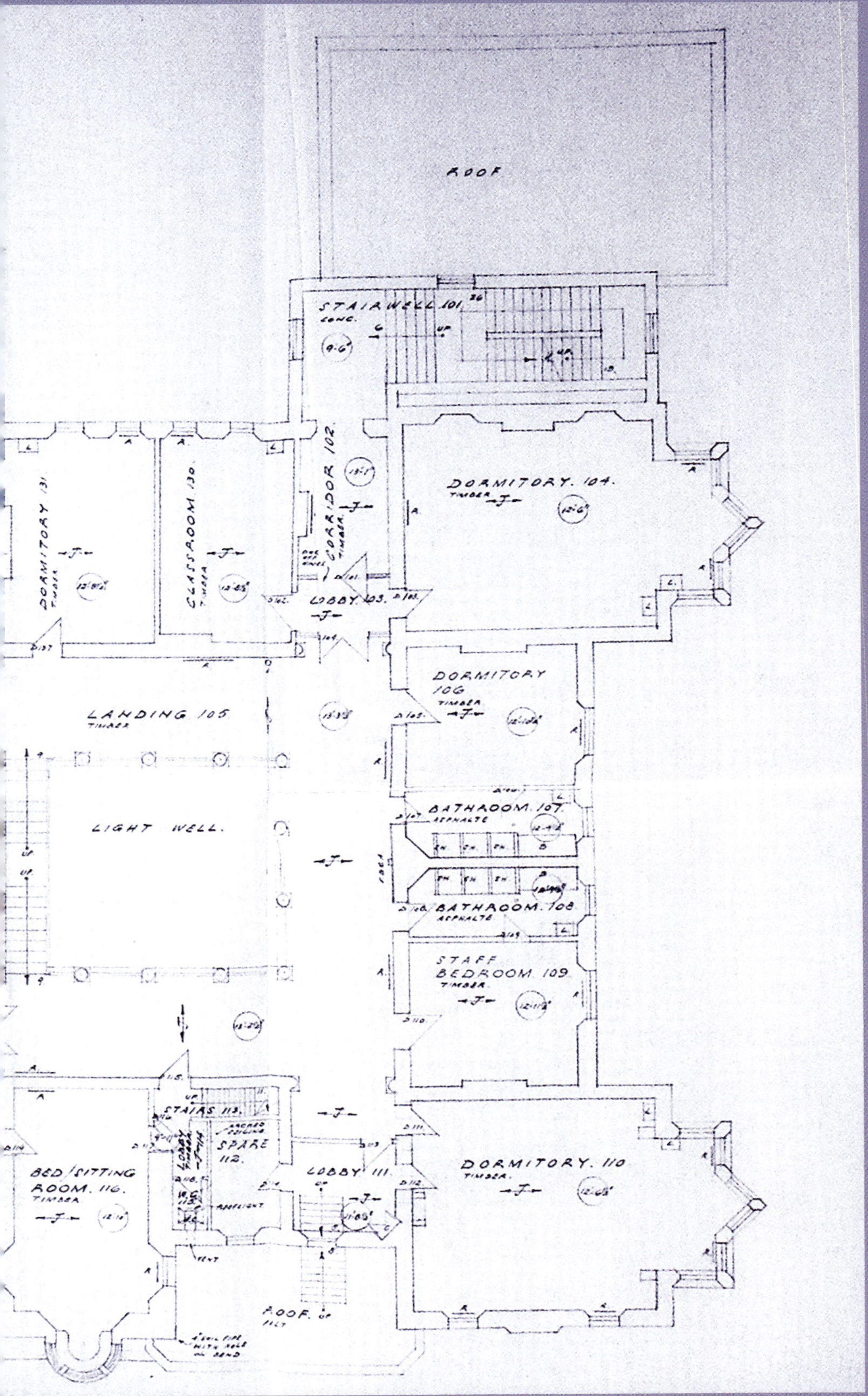
ROOF
STAIRWELL 101.
CONC.
CORRIDOR 102
TIMBER
DORMITORY. 104.
TIMBER
DORMITORY 131
TIMBER
CLASSROOM 130.
TIMBER
LOBBY 103.
LANDING 105.
TIMBER
DORMITORY 106
TIMBER
LIGHT WELL.
BATHROOM. 107.
ASPHALTE
BATHROOM. 108
ASPHALTE
STAFF BEDROOM. 109.
TIMBER
STAIRS 113.
SPARE 112.
LOBBY 111.
BED/SITTING ROOM. 116.
TIMBER
DORMITORY. 110
TIMBER
ROOF.
FELT

An example of changes made
Top picture shows 'improvements' made by removing the conservatory and adding dormers to attic space and the bottom picture is a reminder of Stone Cross in former days

School room in 1950

Inside a dorm

School Dining Hall
(The old Dining Hall - photo on p12 shows it being used for Trafalgar Day Celebrations in 1906)

By 1950 they were ready to open in what was advertised in the opening brochure as, 'a school for sub-normal boys', a title I'm sure would be challenged by today's standards. This consisted of a dormitory boarding school.

Many locals have references to Stone Cross at this time, either through seeing the boys in church, having relatives working there or playing various sports in the grounds.

County line borders became an issue later on and after the school closed it was eventually bought in the 1980s by Marl a local company specialising in the design & manufacture of LED lighting systems.

Typical school photo at the main entrance in the early 1970s

MARL & BEYOND

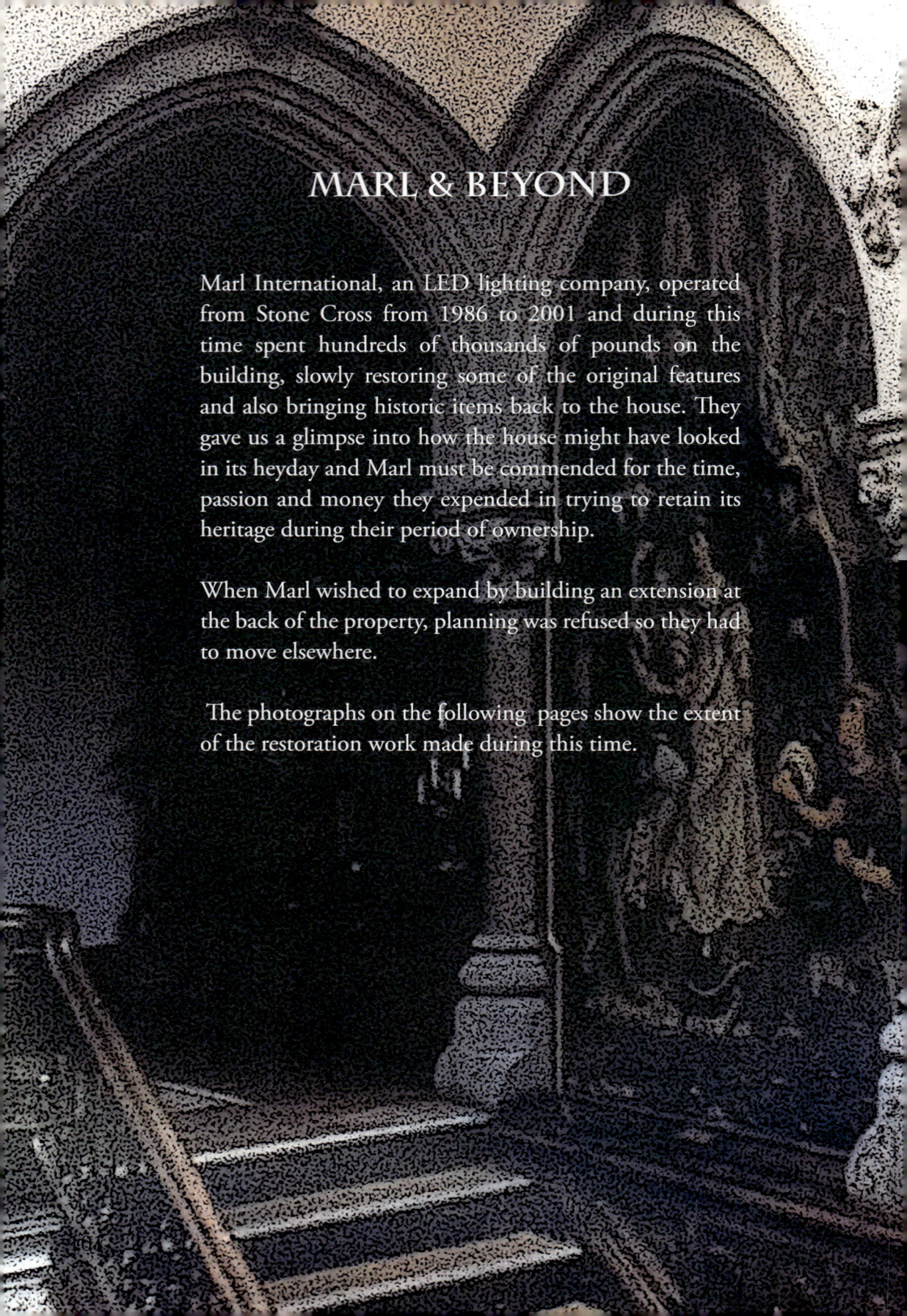

Marl International, an LED lighting company, operated from Stone Cross from 1986 to 2001 and during this time spent hundreds of thousands of pounds on the building, slowly restoring some of the original features and also bringing historic items back to the house. They gave us a glimpse into how the house might have looked in its heyday and Marl must be commended for the time, passion and money they expended in trying to retain its heritage during their period of ownership.

When Marl wished to expand by building an extension at the back of the property, planning was refused so they had to move elsewhere.

The photographs on the following pages show the extent of the restoration work made during this time.

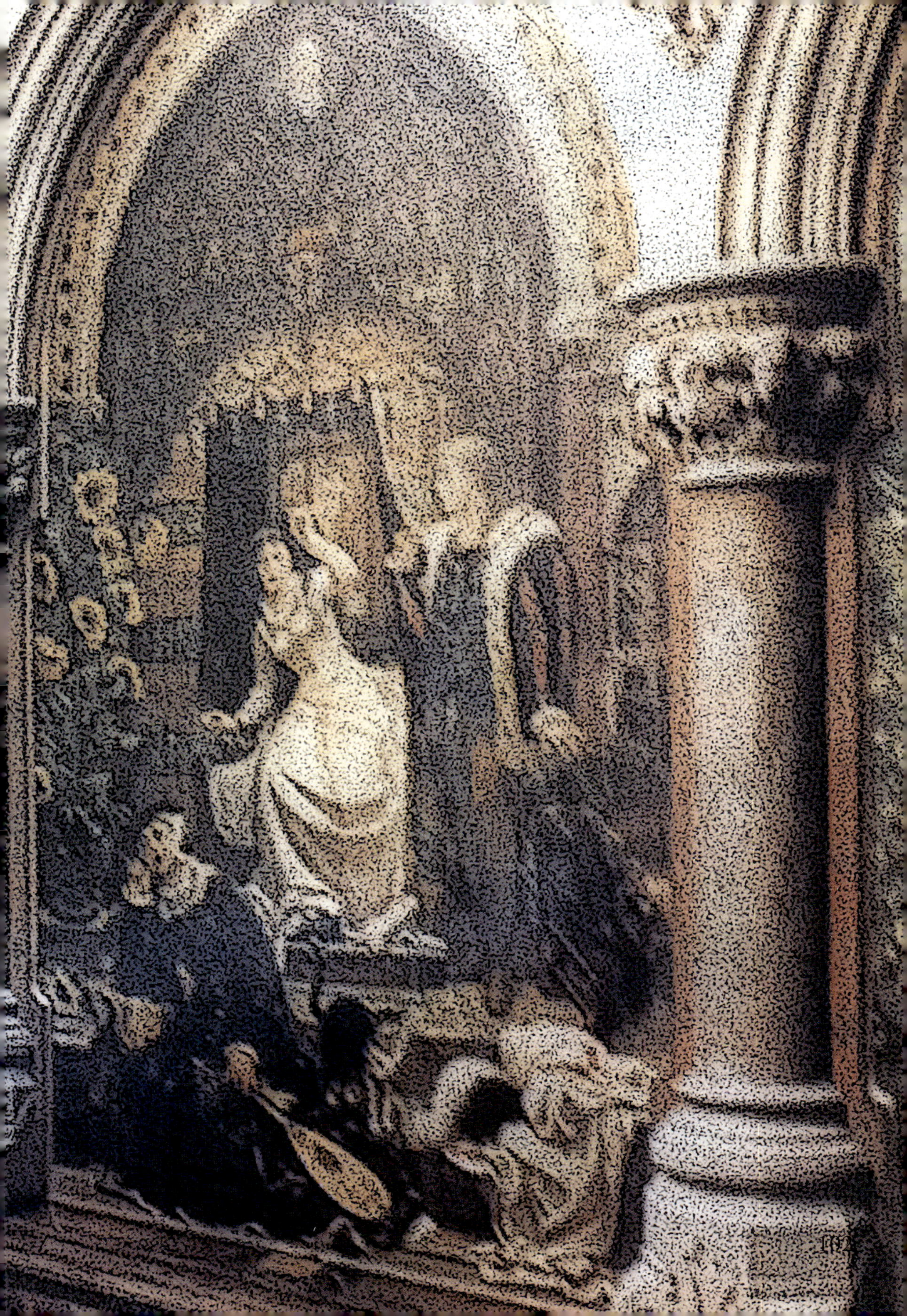

Image courtesy of Marl International

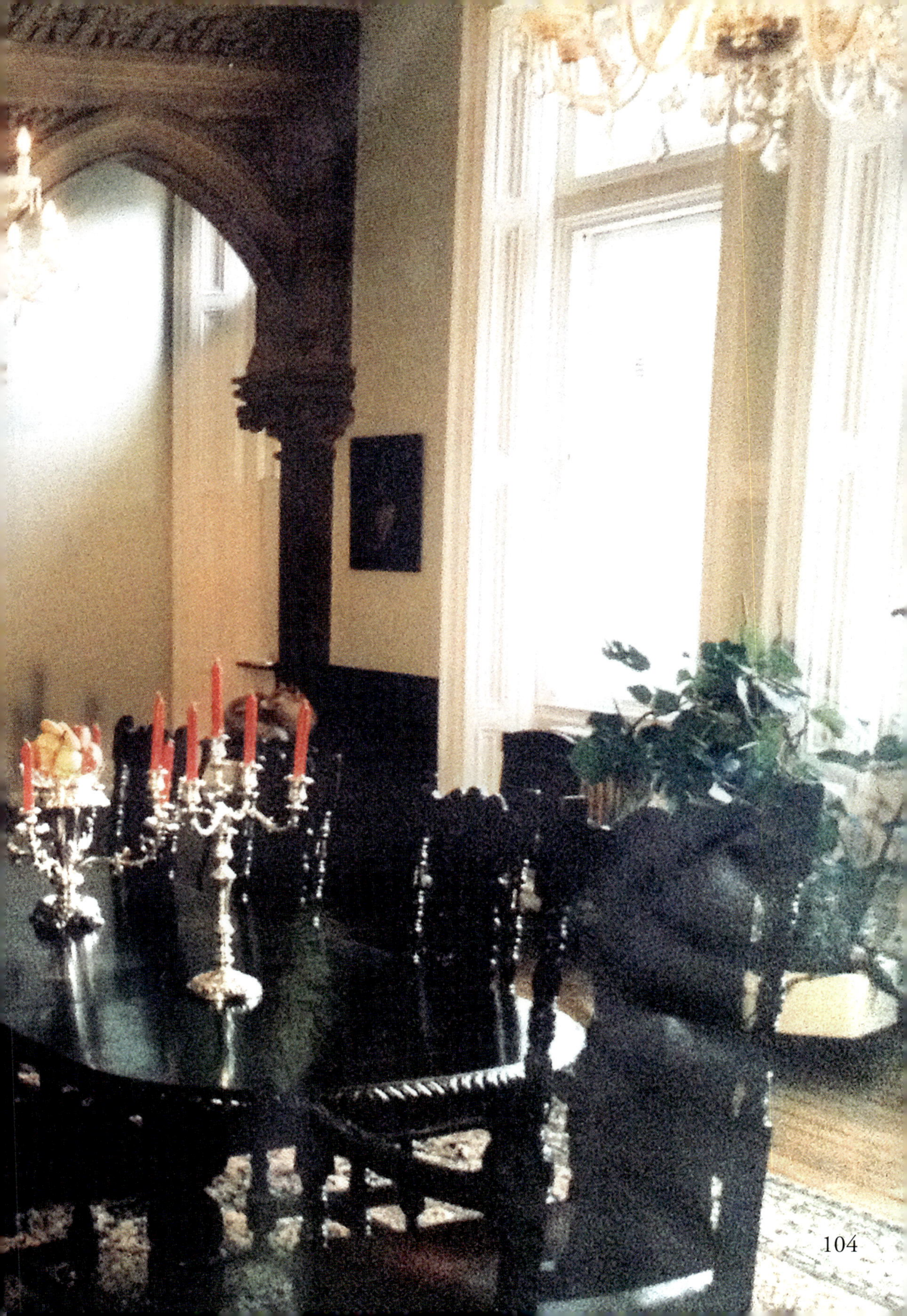

Image courtesy of Marl International

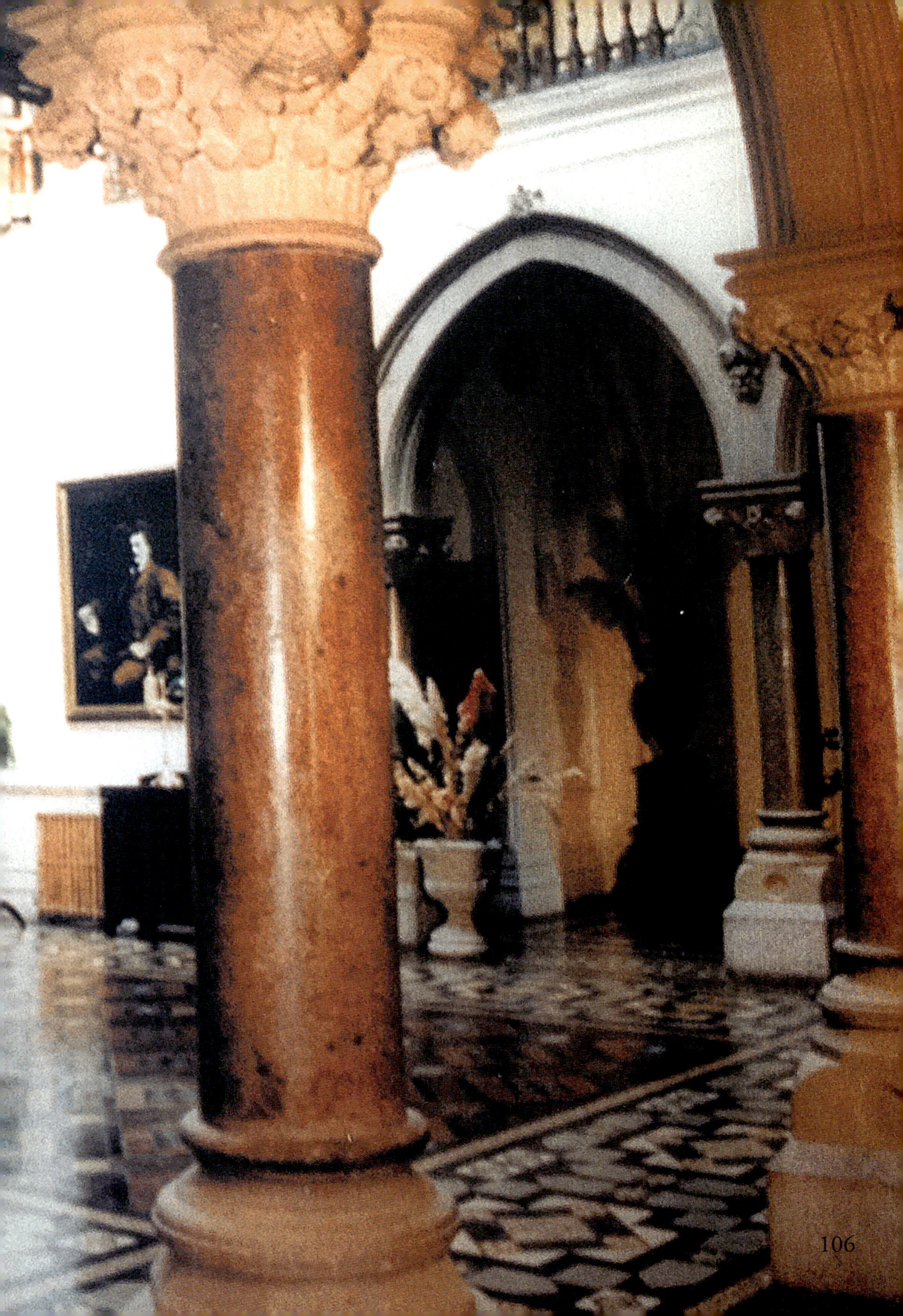

Image courtesy of Marl International

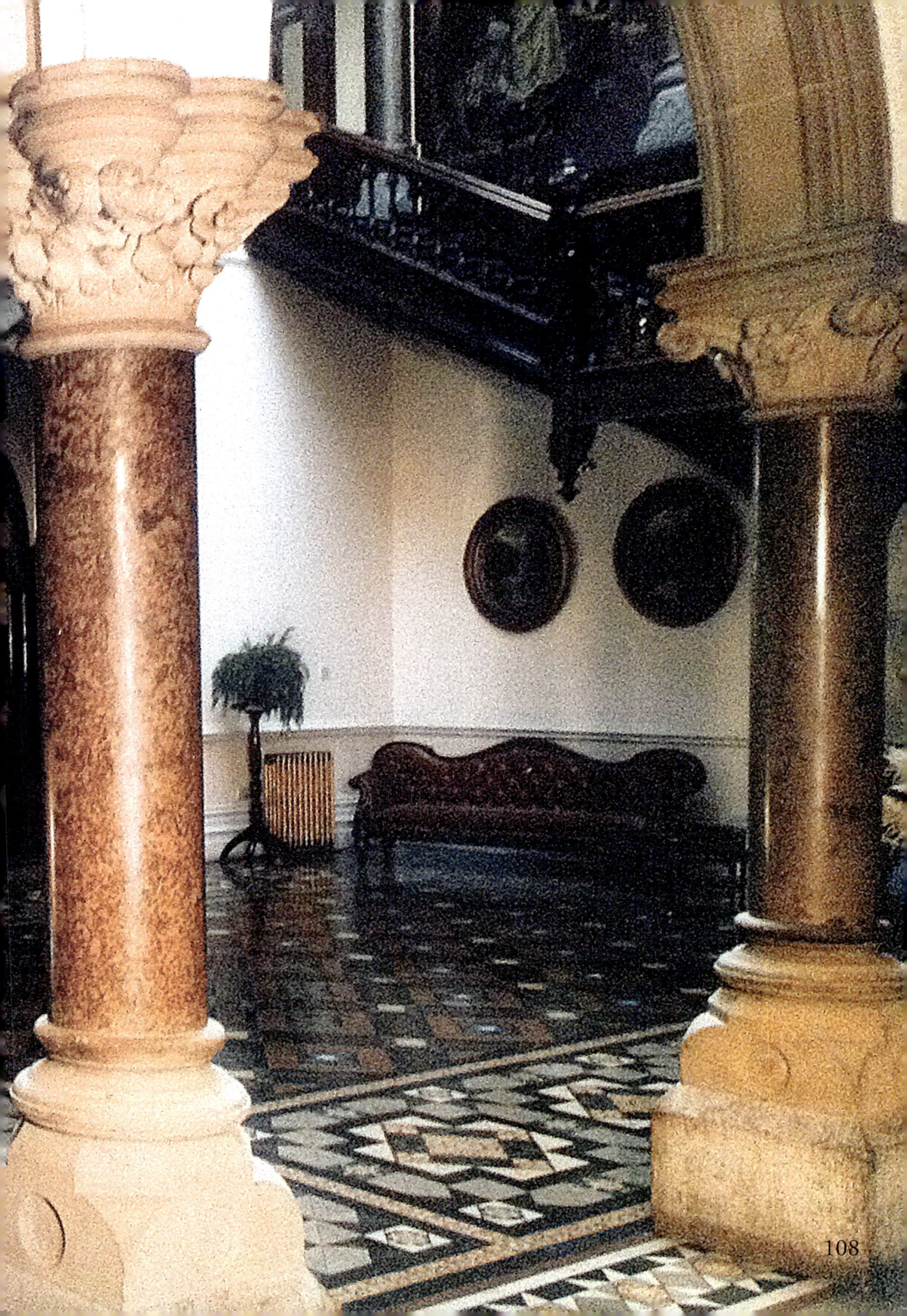

Image courtesy of Marl International

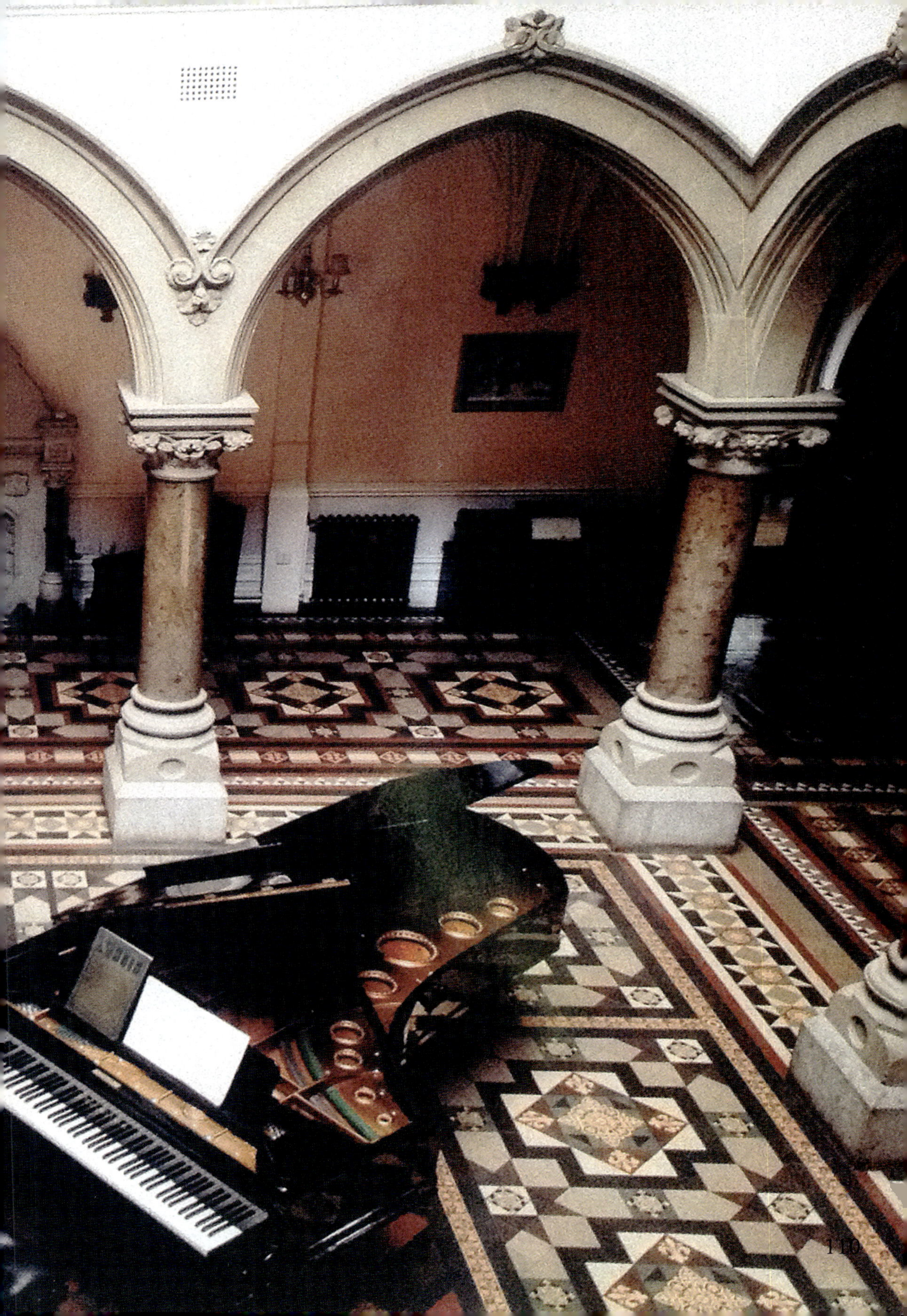

The years after Marl left have not been kind to Stone Cross.

Ownership has passed hands a couple of times and a major fire in 2004 destroyed what would have been the master bedroom and the roof above. This was repaired but other acts of vandalism whilst the building stood empty, included damage to the arch paintings. These have fortunately since been rescued from further damage and have undergone repair work and are held in storage awaiting return to their original position once development works have been completed.

In the years following the fire and subsequent repairs the building has been exposed to further vandalism and trespassing by groups of urban explorers.

This has resulted in the erection of compound fencing around the property with 24 hour security cameras being installed to help protect the building from unwanted guests. The current owners have invested a lot of money to try and stabilise the building's condition in readiness for development.

The present hope for the mansion involves it being converted into 19 apartments and houses to be built in the grounds – which I'm sure will be done sympathetically, and will hopefully lead to the next exciting chapter in the history of Stone Cross Mansion.

KENNEDY COAT OF ARMS

The Kennedys of Hill Foot
ADHAEREO VIRTUTI = ADHERE TO THE POWER

ADHÆREO · VIRTUTI

THE ROWLEY COAT OF ARMS

The coat of arms appears throughout Stone Cross and some examples that survive in stone carvings can still be seen on the house today.

THE KENNEDY COAT OF ARMS

THE KENNEDY COAT OF ARMS

COAT OF ARMS STILL FOUND AT FAIR VIEW

115

KENNEDY GRAVESTONES

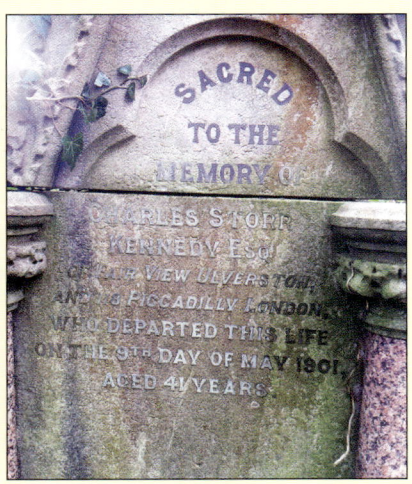

116

Index

A

Ainslie 3, 5, 7, 19, 38, 55, 61, 64
Australia 1, 45, 61, 71, 72, 73

B

Barrow-in-Furness 3, 34, 58
Brockhole 45, 46

C

Cambridge 27, 37
Canada 3, 5, 43, 44
Charles Storr Kennedy 5, 8, 1, 9, 10, 15, 19, 75, 76
Coat of arms 5, 113, 114
Conishead Priory 13, 77
Coronation Hall 25
Croftlands 77

E

Elizabeth Park 9, 1, 2, 9

F

Fair View 5, 1, 2, 9, 13, 15, 29, 75, 90, 115
Ford Park 7
Furness 3, 2, 7, 58, 76

G

Grasmere Sports 25, 26

H

High Sheriff 25, 29
Hill Foot 2, 13, 21, 28, 75, 77, 90, 113
HMS Tobago 47
Holy Trinity 5, 9, 65, 75, 76

J

James Wright Grundy 77

K

Kennedy Bros. 38, 58, 73
Kennedy Cup 27
Kensington 45
King's Own 37

L

Lancashire County Council 27, 90, 91
London 9, 23, 41, 43, 45, 46, 47, 73
Lord Nelson Day 12
Lucien Besche 78

M

Manchester Cathedral 3, 13, 23
Margaret Rowley 6, 9, 3, 13, 19, 22, 38, 40, 41, 44, 45, 49, 51, 55, 60, 64, 67, 69
Marl International 3, 5, 6, 100, 101, 103, 105, 107, 109, 111
Myles Kennedy 5, 6, 1, 3, 4, 13, 19, 30, 61, 76, 77

R

Roanhead 2, 27
Rose Garden 17
Rowley 5, 6, 9, 3, 4, 5, 6, 7, 13, 19, 21, 22, 23, 24, 29, 30, 37, 38, 39, 40, 41, 44, 45, 49, 51, 53, 54, 55, 60, 64, 67, 69, 113
Royal Family 31

S

Sleeping Beauty 78, 84
Stone Cross 5, 6, 1, 12, 13, 14, 15, 16, 19, 23, 34, 37, 38, 41, 64, 75, 76, 77, 78, 87, 89, 90, 97, 100, 101, 111, 112, 114
Stone Cross Mansion 5, 6, 13, 16, 77

T

Trollope 19, 39, 46, 47, 48, 49, 50

U

Ulverston 3, 6, 1, 7, 9, 14, 25, 27, 30, 32, 37, 65, 69, 72, 75, 77
Ulverston Golf Club 25, 27, 30
Ulverston Volunteer Corps 14

W

White Heather II 10, 11
WWI 2, 27, 29, 33, 38, 40, 43, 47, 51, 63
WWII 30, 31, 74, 90